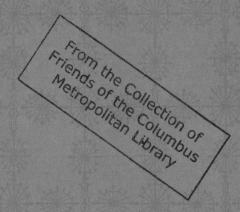

Dear America

The Diary of
Hattie Campbell

Across the Wide
and Lonesome
Prairie

KRISTIANA GREGORY

SCHOLASTIC INC. • NEW YORK

Copyright © 1997 by Kristiana Gregory

All rights reserved. Published by Scholastic Inc., *Publishers since 1920.*
SCHOLASTIC, DEAR AMERICA, and associated logos are trademarks and/or registered
trademarks of Scholastic Inc. No part of this publication may be reproduced,
stored in a retrieval system, or transmitted in any form or by any means,
electronic, mechanical, photocopying, recording, or otherwise, without written
permission of the publisher. For information regarding permission, write to
Scholastic Inc., Attention: Permissions Department,
557 Broadway, New York, NY 10012.

The Library of Congress has cataloged the earlier hardcover edition as follows:
Gregory, Kristiana. Across the Wide and Lonesome Prairie : the Oregon Trail diary of Hattie
Campbell, 1847 / by Kristiana Gregory. p. cm. — (Dear America ; 4) Summary: In her diary,
thirteen-year-old Hattie chronicles her family's arduous 1847 journey from Missouri to Oregon
on the Oregon Trail. ISBN 0-590-22651-7 (alk. paper) 1. Oregon Trail — Juvenile fiction. [1.
Oregon Trail — Fiction. 2. Overland journeys to the Pacific — Fiction. 3. Frontier and pioneer
life — West (U.S.) — Fiction. 4. Diaries — Fiction.] I. Title. II. Series.
PZ7.G8619Pr 1997 [Fic]—dc20 96-25671

This edition ISBN 978-0-545-35066-2

10 9 8 7 6 5 4 3 2 1   12 13 14 15 16

The text type was set in ITC Legacy Serif.
The display type was set in Horley Old Style.
Book design by Kevin Callahan

Printed in the U.S.A. 23
This edition first printing, April 2012

This book about a journey is dedicated, with deep appreciation, to the outstanding editors who have guided and encouraged me along my own journey as a writer: Jeff Fairbanks, Charlie Ferrell, Scott Gray, Regina Griffin, Karen Grove, Tracy Mack, Ann Reit, Art Seidenbaum, and Elinor Williams; most especially to my literary agent and friend, Barbara Markowitz.

Booneville, Missoura

1847

Booneville, Missoura
January 15, 1847, Friday

Sleet and rain.

Ma said that because today is my birthday I may have two slices of chocolate cake. So I did! After supper she gave me a blue satin ribbon for my braid, then when Pa went to bed she let me unwrap another gift. It was a camisole with a matching lace petticoat. Since I'm now thirteen years of age, Ma said it's proper for me to have pretty underthings.

Aunt June agreed, then she gave me this journal. She said every young lady must have a place to record her private thoughts. I will try to do so.

January 20, 1847, Wednesday

Still raining. Our roof is leaking upstairs over the hallway and in my room by the foot of my bed. I've moved the pot there to catch the drips.

I hide this diary under my pillow, but take it out often to look at. I love the smell of its coarse paper and have decided to use my new hair ribbon as a bookmark. The blue looks pretty lying across the page.

February 2, 1847, Tuesday

Three nights ago my poor uncle Milton fell off our roof while he was helping Pa fix a leak. He died right there in the barnyard, there was nothing we could do.

His funeral was today, one of the most interesting days in a very long time. It all started when his coffin fell out the side of our hay wagon and slid down the bank into the river.

Ma held the horses while Pa went after the coffin through the mud and weeds. I hurried after Pa, but my skirt caught in the brush. He grabbed the coffin and had his arms around it to haul it up, but just then a St. Louis steamboat rounded the bend with its big paddles churning up the water and making waves higher than Pa's head. He held on tight, but all of a sudden he floated out into those waves like a cork, me and Ma screaming for help.

Some folks on the top deck yelled until the captain pulled the whistle long and loud. Pa was being sucked into those tall white paddles when someone threw him a rope and pulled him aboard just in time.

We watched the coffin go under. Some moments later it popped free, its lid gone and Uncle Milton, too. Where he went, we don't know, but this is how we came to be acquainted with the riverboat captain who felt so sorry for us that he said he'd take us anywhere we pleased, no charge.

"Anywheres?" Pa asked, as he stomped the water out of his boots.

"Yes, sir," he said. "Anywhere."

This very evening Pa made a shocking announcement: He said that because of the captain's kindness we can now afford to take a riverboat up to Independence, where the Oregon Trail begins. We will take on board our old wagon and our belongings. We will buy some mules in that town, then we will head West.

Just like that.

Ma's mouth dropped open, but no words came out. She was so mad I suspect the next funeral will be my pa's.

February 3, 1847, Wednesday

Wind blowing through this creaky old house kept me awake most of the night, so here I am in my shawl, looking out the little window by my bed, trying to stay warm. Since my room is in the attic it stays cold until Ma opens the stair door. My fingers are numb, so I will write quick.

I can hear Ma downstairs frying up bacon and putting coffee on. She did not speak to Pa the rest of yesterday, nor has she this morning, for all I hear is silence after Pa's questions.

When Ma gets mad, she stays mad a long time.

February 5, 1847, Friday

Three days have gone by with Ma only speaking to me, my little brothers, and Aunt June. Finally at supper tonight she looked at Pa and said, "Charles Campbell, Oregon is two thousand miles away."

Pa nodded. He seemed so relieved to have Ma talking again. She said, "Tell me why, Charles, and I will tell you yes or no."

My, it was a long evening. I took up the plates and set to washing them with Jake. He is six and likes to splash the water, but still he is a help. Bennie's two so he stayed on Ma's knee while she listened to Pa.

Pa said he'd been unhappy about so many people settling here in Missoura. It's crowded. Taxes are high. And there's swamp fever that kills folks every summer.

At the mention of swamp fever Pa grew quiet. He swallowed hard, then looked at Ma with tears in his eyes. In a soft voice he said her name: "Augusta," he said, "we'll be able to start a new life, where there ain't no sad memories. There's space out West, all the land we want. Free for the taking. Winters are mild, that's what these pamphlets say."

He held up a booklet called *The Emigrants' Guide, to Oregon and California* by Lansford W. Hastings, and another by the explorers John C. Frémont and Kit Carson.

I took my candle upstairs. I'm not sure if Ma said yes or no, but I'm happy to once again hear them whispering together in their room.

February 7, 1847, Sunday

We have given up hope of finding Uncle Milton's body. So today in church folks took turns walking up to the pulpit to say a few kind words. My friend Becky, she's exactly my age, she sang a hymn so sweet all the ladies dabbed hankies to their cheeks.

Afterward my aunt June and uncle Tim came in a freezing rain and we sat together in front of the fire. I served up coffee and two peach pies made from last summer's preserves. My, it was delicious. When they said they wanted to come to

Oregon, too, well, Mama smiled for the first time in days for Aunt June is her dear younger sister. (It was their brother, Milton, that died.)

February 9, 1847, Tuesday

Word spreads fast in a small town. Everyone's talking about Oregon and California.

Becky says she would positively perish from loneliness if I left Booneville, which is where we were born and have lived our whole lives. "Please don't go, Hattie," she said. "If you leave Missoura, we may never see each other again." I feel sad when Becky talks so.

It's pretty much divided down the middle who thinks which is the best place to go to.

Pa said that since California is like a foreign country and we don't speak Spanish we best head for Oregon. It's occupied by the British, but at least those folks speak English.

Our new president is James Polk. Pa says the only reason he won the election is because he promised to make Oregon and California territories of the United States. So if enough of us get up and go, it'll help push the foreigners aside for good.

It's our "Manifest Destiny," according to President Polk. It's our responsibility to spread democracy all the way to the Pacific coast.

Ma was at her mending this morning, in the window seat where the light is good. I sat on the little stool with the embroidered cushion. When I looked up, I saw she was crying.

"What is it, Mama?"

She lifted the hem of her apron to dry her cheeks. "Hattie, I don't care about 'Manifest Destiny.' The West is wilderness. It'll be a frightfully long journey with no turning back. All our dear friends live in Booneville, and besides, I don't think I can bear to leave behind your sisters."

I lay my face on Ma's lap. She was talking about my four sweet sisters, three older, one younger. Last summer—the most horrible summer of our lives—they died one right after the other, from swamp fever, and they are buried next to my grandparents under the big walnut tree out back.

I am now the eldest of the Campbell children. I am thirteen years of age and am afraid of only four things in the whole world.

1. Indians
2. copperhead snakes
3. a toothache
4. losing my little brothers, Ben and Jake, they're all I got now

February 18, 1847, Thursday

Yesterday Aunt June received another letter from her friend Narcissa Whitman, who went to Oregon ten years ago. Her husband is Dr. Marcus Whitman and they have founded a mission near Fort Walla Walla to help the Cayuse Indians. Aunt June had us to tea; Becky, too. She let us girls pour and pass around the scones and butter so that she could read the letter aloud. This much I remember:

There is tall timber and soil so rich a farm can grow overnight it seems. June, you'll see how fair is the climate. If I can cross the Rockies, any lady can.

Aunt June folded the letter into her sleeve. She said Narcissa and Eliza Spalding were the first white women to travel all the way to Oregon. There've been hundreds since, hundreds. We could visit her, maybe even stay awhile since Narcissa's been begging us to come for years.

Aunt June is not at all sad to leave Booneville. She thinks everything is an adventure and (I'm writing this in tiny letters so no one can read over my shoulder) she confided to me that the way their brother Milton's coffin went sailing down the Missoura was "Splendid! The best amusement in months."

Aunt June and I think alike.

March 4, 1847, Thursday

Two weeks of packing and sewing and cooking and repacking. We leave aboard the riverboat *Eliza May*, in just ten days.

TEN DAYS!

Pa sold our house and our chickens, our three horses and our cow to a neighbor for $65 — this plus $800 is what we'll take to Oregon. (Having free tickets is what finally gave Pa the courage to say we're going.)

Every evening we visit with friends or relations for supper and tearful good-byes. Suddenly I realize how much I shall miss Becky—we have known each other since we were babies and when we walk together down the lane I get a terrible lump in my throat knowing we'll soon be parted. She is my very best friend ever.

Pa is ready to get going, but Ma is gathering keepsakes from each friend and packets of seeds saved from their gardens. One whole trunk is filled with my sisters' things—a favorite doll and dress each, baby knits and such—Ma's wedding dress and my grandparents' Bible and washbasin.

Pa said, "Are you sure we need all this?" Ma, tight-lipped and teary, said nothing. She just kept on folding quilts and tucking a china dish or bowl or picture frame between the folds.

I am allowed a small satchel. There is space for a folded dress, leggings, my hairbrush, two petticoats, and this-and-that. My journal will fit in the side pocket with three pencils. Aunt June says I must record things daily—the good and the bad—because this will be the adventure of my lifetime.

"Hattie, whether you realize it or not, we will be part of history."

March 15, 1847, Monday
Aboard the Steamboat *Eliza May*

We are fifteen miles west of Booneville, finally. Our first day out we got stuck on a sandbar until the tide floated us off.

I am sitting on a bench on the top deck and can see all around for miles. There are trees everywhere and tiny houses along dirt roads.

There is such a breeze up here that I've had to tie my bonnet tight under my chin. I am writing quick because I must get back to help Ma with Bennie and Jake. If I lean over the rail I can see them on the lower deck among our baggage. Pa and the other men are tightening ropes around the wagons, for they were taken apart before loading. Nearby, our wagon wheels are stacked like hotcakes.

Already I'm lonesome for Becky.

March 16, Tuesday

The *Eliza May* is packed with travelers, some from clear down in Kentucky and Tennessee, who've been aboard for days and days. A lady in the cabin next to us was sick all night, but it turns out she was just having a baby. It was born at sunrise, a tiny little girl they named Eliza May.

I ain't never heard of a baby being named after a riverboat. The mother and father already have five young daughters and they are all named after trees! I wonder if the family will fit in one wagon all the way to Oregon.

I write this from my berth. An oil lamp gives light as Ma changes Bennie for bed. Jake is tucked in with Pa, and even though Pa is snoring, Jake keeps asking questions about Indians and scalpings, buffalo, and other things he wants to see out West. He's as ready for our adventure as I am.

There . . . I've just covered him up and whispered a prayer to him. He fell fast asleep before I finished. Ma is so tired.

March 25, Thursday
Independence, Missoura

Pa said there must be 500 folks living here, and that don't count all the emigrants like us roaming the streets, buying last-minute supplies, repairing wagons, and just plain getting ready. There are blacksmiths, harness makers, and wheelwrights busy morning and night.

After we docked it took one full day and evening for men to unload the *Eliza May*. First thing Pa and Uncle Tim did was put the wheels back on our wagons, load our trunks, furniture, and tools, then find a boy who could help us buy some mules.

I am writing this on my lap by the campfires as I keep an eye on Ma's roasting chicken. It is on a low spit over the coals we're sharing with another family. Behind me are the houses and barns and stores and streets of Independence.

But in front of me, it's open prairie, miles and miles of grass spread out like Ma's old yellow quilt. There are dozens of families with tents and wagons also camped here, looking westward.

Pa says we are waiting for the grass to green-up. When there is green grass, why then we'll be able to feed the horses and other animals pulling us west.

Pa is patient, but I ain't. The stench from there being no outhouses gets worse every day. Oh, I wish we could just get on with things.

March 30, Tuesday

Rain. Roads are so muddy most of the emigrants are staying around their fires in camp. We have made friends with three families who are also bound for Oregon. We hung tarps between the wagon tops and now have a dry space in between where Ma and the other ladies sit with babies and needlework.

It is no fun just sitting, sitting, sitting. How I

wish Becky was here so we could roam together.

There are many boys my age and older. They have made a sport of shoving each other into puddles and wrestling in the mud. Four boys jumped on the back of a poor old milk cow and tried to ride her through camp. When her calf came bawling after her there was near a stampede.

I don't like the way these boys yell and wave their rifles around. One of them accidentally shot a nine-year-old in the neck. He died quick, right where he fell. His family is so brokenhearted they have packed up and headed home to St. Louis. I'm sad for them.

Now I keep a closer eye on Jake and Ben. If they got shot I think I'd take a whip and make those rough boys sorry they was ever born.

Aunt June made the acquaintance of a family going to San Francisco. They have twins, a boy and a girl about six years old. It seems we'll all start out together and somewhere in the Cheyenne country when the trail splits, some of us will head north and the others south to California.

April 5, Monday

Bad news swept through camp this morning like a fever, news brung by mountain men back from the West. Ma looked so upset I feared she was ill.

"Maybe we should go home, back to Booneville," she said to Pa. "There's just too much danger . . . I cannot lose another one of my children, Charles."

Even the men are talking among themselves. This is what I heard:

An emigrant train that left Independence last spring got trapped in a blizzard high in the Sierra Nevada Mountains near California. Forty-some people froze or starved to death. To stay alive, folks ate their livestock, their pets, and then — this is the worst part — they ate parts of their dead friends! These were the Reed and Donner families and some were rescued just this February. A whole winter in the mountains without food or shelter or warm clothes — how they must have suffered!

Word is that they took the Hastings Cutoff, but something went wrong somehow. Ma is worried because the written guide we are following is also Hastings's. What if his maps are wrong for us, too? She is by the fire with Pa, pleading for him to turn back.

I must be brave for Bennie and Jake, and I must be brave for Ma. But what if something happens to us and we can't get over the mountains in time?

April 6, Tuesday

Pa went into town to trade our mules for oxen. A mountain man in furs named Tall Joe told us the grain that mules eat is expensive and takes up room in the wagons. Oxen are better because they eat grass along the trail and are so slow Indians won't steal them.

Tall Joe said, "Whatever y'folks do, hurry along as fast as y'can and don't take shortcuts like them Donners did." People crowd around asking advice: "What about Indians?" or "What about crossing the desert?"

On Tall Joe's belt he has what looks like two short brushes hanging with a string of beads. Ma was admiring the beadwork and reached out to touch them when Tall Joe said proudly, "Them is scalps, ma'am . . . Pawnee."

Ma's hand flew up to her throat. Before she could gather herself, the little twins and my brother Jake leaned forward for a better look. Jake said, just as calm as if he was asking for lunch, "Did the Injuns yell when you scalped 'em, mister?"

"No, sonny, jest when I shot 'em."

Then Tall Joe lay down by his fire with three of his friends. They fell asleep so quick, they looked like old rugs rolled up.

I stared at the scalps.

Indians?

April 7, Wednesday

The Anderson family is camped near us — the one with baby Eliza May and her five tree sisters. I get them mixed up, but here's the names anyhow: Hazel, Holly, Laurel, Olive, and Cassia. Cassia is about two years old and has hair the color of cinnamon. She has taken a liking to me, I think, because she comes and sits on my lap whenever I'm holding Bennie.

The baby, Eliza May, cries night and day with a high-pitched wail that reminds me of a steamboat whistle. When Mrs. Anderson greeted me yesterday morning after a long and loud night, I said (in a nice way, I thought) that it's a good thing she named her baby after a steamboat because she sure did sound like one.

Well, Mama overheard and said I must apologize for being rude. It's not nice to make fun of people, she said, especially their habits or names.

There's a dance most every evening on account of there are plenty of fiddlers and foot-stompers. Ma said it's so pleasant and folks're so friendly, she'd be content to camp here all summer then go home. Home to Booneville.

April 12, Monday

Pa says any day now the grass'll start greening and we must be ready to go. Some of the men are trying to pick leaders, but there are so many arguments about who will be boss and what the rules will be, Pa says we'll just move on out with Tall Joe as he seems to be the most experienced.

Our wagon is so handsome you wouldn't guess it used to be our old farm rig. Pa and Uncle Tim added six tall hoops to hold the canvas on top. It looks as plump and white as a fresh-raised loaf of bread.

Inside it's neatly packed, but crowded. Our boxes of food, dishes, and pots are in back to make cooking quicker, tools and furniture are in front with our barrel of water. In the middle, between sacks of flour and beans, is a small nest where I can sit with the boys. Two lanterns hang from the hoops, along with extra coils of rope, our canteens, tin pans, and tin cups. It is noisy as a tinker's cart.

There's not one spare inch for anyone to stretch out inside, so every night we must pitch tents . . . one for Ma and Pa, the other I'm to share with Bennie and Jake. Ours fits like a lean-to alongside the wagon and is cozy and out of the wind. Still, I'm bothered to sleep outside for the next six months. What about snakes? What if Indians come in the middle of the night?

April 14, Wednesday

I have made a friend! She is fourteen, one year older than I am, with freckles over her nose and cheeks, and beautiful green eyes. She is not as bossy as Becky, matter-of-fact she seems real shy, but I think I shall like her very much anyhow.

When I told her I am scared of Indians she said, "Don't worry, Hattie, there are probably plenty more good Indians than bad." We have been walking to the edge of town together, to watch the blacksmith repair tools and such. My friend's name is Pepper Lewis and she has a twin brother named Wade.

Camped near us is a lady who is so fat she can barely walk; she must weigh 300 pounds. Her arms are as thick as my waist. It is hard not to stare, especially on account of that her husband has no legs. Either she carries him around or he rides in a little cart she pulls. I hope they don't come over to visit with Ma because I won't know what to say.

April 22, Thursday
Alcove Spring

We are three days west of Independence, camped at Alcove Spring. Water gushes from a ledge, down ten feet into a pool where there are ferns and deep shade. How delicious the water tastes! Ma and I waited our turn with other women in the wagon train to fill our canteens and jugs. A tiny frog swam into my palm, then out again—all the while we were serenaded by crickets.

My feet are sore and blistered, so much that it hurts to walk. It felt good to soak them in the cool pond. I want to go barefoot, but Mama says there are too many stickers and thorns. Soon enough the blisters will turn to calluses, she said.

When we finally pulled out of Independence, leaving behind the Missoura River, the sun wasn't up yet. Two dozen wagons were already ahead of us. Behind were hundreds of cows, horses, and sheep. I was so excited I yelled, "Hooray, hooray!" At long last we were on our way to Oregon.

But, oh, the dust! So much dust, we could barely see the rumps of our own oxen. My eyes stung and we all were coughing.

Pa steered to one side of the trail, but other families pulled alongside, making four abreast. I soon tired of the bumping and jolting and rattling, and sitting in a cramped space, so I gathered my skirt about my knees and jumped to the ground.

I ran between the wagons until I saw Pepper sitting up with her pa. I hollered to her. When she leapt down her skirt flew up, showing off her leggings, white as cattails. We hurried away from the trail where it wasn't as noisy.

We walked for six hours and talked the whole time! She said, "Hattie, when we get to Oregon let's ask our fathers to build houses right next door to each other." And I said, "Then we can share a garden. I'll plant the lettuce and corn, you plant tomatoes." So as we walked along, Pepper and I planned out our whole future, down to the matching lace curtains we'd make for our bedrooms, the pet kittens we'd raise, and so on.

My, how the dust leaves a gritty taste in our mouths. It is awful. With every step our hems pick up burrs from the tall grass, dried brush scratches our ankles. Finally that first day, when the sun was directly overhead, everyone stopped. Pepper and I were so wore out, we fell back into the shade of our wagon, laughing.

"Do we have to keep going?" we asked Pa. He just smiled at us as he carried water to the animals.

The first night camping was a late one with singing and dancing. Pepper and I swung in a circle with Jake and the little twins, 'round and 'round.

We are on our way! was the cry heard over and over. Even Ma joined in when folks started singing "Buffalo Gals," but when Pa asked her to do-si-do she lifted Bennie onto her hip and turned for the wagon.

"Time for bed," she said. Maybe when Mama sees Oregon, she will dance.

April 25, Sunday

At 4 o'clock in the morning, when it is still pitch-dark, the bugle sounds. This is when breakfast fires are started and men ride out to herd in the animals, but today there was a loud discussion. Some families want to rest because of the Sabbath, for prayer and worship. But some, including Pa, say we must press on with no delays. Winter could come early and we need to be over the mountains by then. We must not make the same mistake as the Donners.

No one says much about them, but I often think about the terrible, terrible business of eating dead friends. I'm brave, but not near brave enough to do that.

So we must hurry along. October is six months away. Will it really take half a year to reach Oregon? I wonder.

Finally, just before sunrise, the men agreed to travel on Sundays, but families will take turns reading Scripture and giving a prayer at each meal.

The prairie is wide and lonesome without a house or barn in sight. We caught up to several heavy freight wagons drawn by mules. Pa said we are on the Santa Fe Trail. In a few miles the trail will split: The freighters will head southwest toward the Territory of Mexico and we shall continue northwest.

With every mile it feels like the sky and trail are moving with us, as if we're walking in place. Everything looks the same no matter how far we've come. Only when I look down at my dusty shoes and see that, yes, I am walking forward and the footprints behind are mine, can I believe that we are actually moving.

Girls are gathering dandelions in their aprons to make a salad, also young leaves from tumbleweed plants. Aunt June said to look for wild carrots and onions from seeds dropped by last summer's travelers. The little twins found sunflower stalks and pretended to ride them like ponies. They are such dear children, I shared some taffy with them at supper.

April 27, Tuesday

A few days ago we crossed the Kansas River. At first I was scared watching the horses wade in because water splashed their heads, and I worried they wouldn't be able to breathe. But somehow they managed to swim, paddling like dogs, their necks stretched high and strong.

Now we are at the Big Blue River, which is much wider and faster than the Kansas. The men are discussing how we should cross it, and whether we should do so now before dark. Everyone is dead tired. Most families want to spend the night on this side because there's plenty of dry firewood and they want to rest.

One lady yelled out, "We are wore out, mister. Can't you see that?"

But Tall Joe just stood high on a wagon seat and held up his arms for quiet. "We gotta cross now," he shouted back. He said the river's low, but it could rise overnight, no tellin'. Another thing he said, come tomorrow morning the animals will be so frisky they'll be harder to force into the water.

I must help Ma wrap up the cheese and figs we ate at noon, and change Bennie's wet pants. Already two men are riding to the other side. Water is up to their saddles and the horses' tails are floating. Several boys on horseback are whooping and yelling as they ride across. Their rifles were taken away from them so they wouldn't shoot anybody by mistake. Hooray.

April 2?, Wednesday, I think

While crossing the Big Blue, Jake, Bennie, and I sat in our little spot in the wagon. As we floated I could feel the pull and jerk as the animals struggled to swim. We could see forward through a small space between boxes. There were many wagons ahead of us, their white tops swaying from the current.

Suddenly Pa jumped into the river to turn our oxen because they were trying to swim downstream. Ma grabbed the reins and wrapped them around her hands.

When we began tipping over on our right side

I screamed, terrified we'd sink. Water poured in through the canvas. I could see that Ma's bonnet had fallen back over her shoulders and she was pulling the reins hard, trying to turn the animals. Everything in the wagon not tied down slid toward us. Two sacks of beans rolled onto my legs and a bag of flour burst open when it fell against the rocker.

While looking straight ahead, Ma yelled for us to lean with all our weight against the high wall. As we clung to an overhead hoop one of the lanterns swung and hit my head so hard I wanted to let go, but I knew I must keep my arm around little Ben so he wouldn't get washed away.

Pa kept swimming with the oxen and with Ma's help, we somehow tipped back up. It seemed forever, but was probably just a minute.

Bennie was crying because he was scared and his clothes were wet. The three of us were covered with a gooey white paste from the spilled flour. It felt awful. My sleeves were sticky and my braid was stiff as a broom.

Finally there was a thump as our wheels

touched bottom, then there was splashing as our team pulled us through the mud and onto the beach. More water rushed in, soaking our blankets, but we've hung them over brush to dry while we wait on shore for the others. It might take two days to get everyone across.

I hope we don't have to cross any more rivers!

This afternoon my little friends the twins wandered off to pick berries, but now it is near sunset and they've not returned. Their parents are frantic and I'm worried sick. Tall Joe and Pa are leading a search party. I wanted to help, too, but Ma said she needs me to watch Jake and Bennie so she can go sit with the twins' mother, to comfort her.

Oh, those poor children — they're much too small to be lost.

Next day

When the bugle sounded at 4 o'clock, I awoke with a sick feeling, remembering I'd fallen asleep to the voices of worried adults. Some had taken torches beyond the corral of wagons to search the grass and riverbanks, late into the night.

When I crawled out from the quilt, Bennie and Jake rolled sleepily into my warm space.

"Mama?" I called.

"I'm here, Hattie." Her voice came from her tent.

"Have the little twins been found?" I whispered.

Ma stepped out of the doorway. Dark circles were under her eyes, and her braid was over her shoulder, not combed out since yesterday.

"No, dear, they ain't been found."

Ma hurried us through breakfast of cold biscuits and jam. When Pa brought in the oxen and began harnessing them, I cried out, "We can't be leaving!"

He and Ma looked at each other. "Two other families will stay behind to help the parents search, Hattie. We must keep going."

"But why? Why can't we stay and help, too?"

Pa came over and put his strong arms around me. "I'm sorry the children are lost, Hattie. But their ma and pa have insisted that everyone keep going. They understand we can't all stay. I'm sorry."

As we pulled out I watched the campsite. The mother was just a small shape until we rounded a bluff, then I saw her no more.

I pulled my brothers into my lap and started to sing them a song, but my heart was so heavy I burst out crying.

Later

I taught Jake how to shake out his blanket, then roll it up with string. I must do Bennie's because he just drags his in the dust. Ma is too tired to notice their dirty faces so I wash them myself.

Another day

Today we came to the Little Blue, but thank God we didn't have to cross it. Our wagons are so heavy, the oxen strain to pull us up the trail. We'll follow the river into Nebraska.

Every time we stop and the dust has settled, I look back to see if the little twins and their family have caught up. No one speaks of them and I don't know why.

This morning I made batter for pancakes. I went to the stream to fill my pitcher, but when I returned to camp the batter was black with mosquitoes. I started to dump it into the dirt, but Aunt June put her hand on my arm.

"Hattie," she said, "don't waste — just stir them up good. The griddle's hot enough to cook 'em through and no one ever died from such."

So we had mosquitoes for breakfast. Jake called them "skeeter cakes" and he said they tasted just fine soaked in molasses, but to me they were like sand in my teeth.

When we opened one of our sacks we found the bacon to be green and crawling with maggots, fifty pounds of it. Ma was so furious she shouted at my father.

"That butcher in Independence said it would last months and look here," she said to Pa, wiping her finger along the meat. "There ain't a lick of salt anywhere." Every day it seems there is a new disappointment for my poor mother.

Jake thought it was all right by him if we cooked up some maggots, but Pa dragged the sack outside of camp and buried it.

At least three other families were sold rotten meat also.

Three days later

I have lost track of days and dates so from now on shall not worry about them. Aunt June has also lost track because she's been sick with dizziness. Uncle Tim drives while she lies in the wagon, the canvas sides rolled up from the bottom to let air in. Ma herself is tired and grouchy. She says the dust gives her a headache something fierce.

There's no sign of the little twins' family.

A lady by the name of Mrs. Kenker brought over a cup of soup last night, but Aunt June was too vomitty to even taste it. Mrs. Kenker has gray hair wrapped on top her head and she has all her teeth. She smiled real pretty and asked "how y'be" to everyone; she reminds me of my sweet old grandma.

She and her husband are well liked, it seems. At night when the fiddler starts up, they lead out with a waltz or polka, depending on how slow or fast the music. Soon the married couples join in, then the younger men with sweethearts.

"How lovely they are together," folks whisper about Mr. and Mrs. Kenker.

But I know something folks don't.

This morning before sunrise, as we were taking down our tent, Mrs. Kenker came to check on Aunt June, so sweet and gentle-like. She lay her hand on my aunt's forehead then kissed her cheek. Then just as smooth and quiet as you please, Mrs. Kenker reached into our cooking box and slipped one of Ma's silver spoons into her apron pocket!

I thought my eyes was playing tricks on me. My mouth dropped open, but no words came out.

What will Mama do if I tell her?

Evening

When we reached the high grassland of Indian country we saw wide-open prairie filled with wildflowers, yellow, blue, and red, like patches on a quilt. Tall Joe says that some days ahead we'll meet up with emigrants coming down from Iowa and Wisconsin Territory. There could be twice as many of us then, all heading west.

Pa wonders if there will be enough grass for all our animals or enough firewood for our camps.

I've decided to walk to Oregon on account of there is no comfortable way to ride. Our rocking chair broke when it fell out the back and Ma insists on keeping it even though Pa says it takes up more room broke. She is so cross with him, she will not listen to reason. And I don't want to upset her even more by telling about her stolen spoon.

All day our wagon drove alongside the Anderson family with baby Eliza May and her tree sisters (Mama says I must stop calling them that). How their mother cleans Eliza May's and Cassia's diapers is an amazing sight:

After breakfast she pins them with thorns to the canvas sides of their wagon. As they flap in the breeze they dry and the sun bleaches them whiter than they were hours before. By noon, there are more tacked to each side, and just before we turn into a circle at sundown, the Anderson wagon looks like a creature with many tiny wings.

Pepper and I and some other girls hunted for food near old campsites. She has such a pleasant way of giving orders that several younger girls tagged along, eager to look here or there, and dig in the dirt with their fingers.

"Like this, Pepper?" they asked, and she would pat them on their shoulders and say, "Why, yes, that's perfect. Good work." After a couple of hours we had found small red potatoes, some pearl onions, and rosemary.

Next day

Our train has about 135 wagons, so at night we divide into groups, spread out over a couple miles. For the past week we've had the same 23 wagons in our circle. The littlest children can play safe inside while mothers gather around the fire to cook or visit. We are all becoming well acquainted.

This is how we pull into a circle: The tongue

of our wagon rests near the inside rear wheel of Uncle Tim's and his does the same with the wagon in front of him and so forth. All the wagons together form a horseshoe with an opening about 20 feet wide so folks can come and go.

After the animals are unhitched they are let out to pasture with the rest of the stock. Men take turns guarding so in case of an Indian attack they are ready to herd them into our corral and pull chains across for a gate. Thus far we ain't seen any Indians and I'm glad for that.

(Folks say they are dirty and vicious, but I don't know.)

Ma is more cheerful today, but Pa still avoids arguing with her. She's been caring for Aunt June and this morning said the illness was on account of Aunt June going to have a baby! Before we get to Oregon!

Two large kettles are on the fire tonight—one with beans and the other with vegetables and beef bones left over from last night's meal. Some families spread a cloth in the dirt to make it look nice, but us—Ma and Aunt June—are already sick of washing dishes so sometimes we just take turns dipping cups in and sharing spoons, then it's not so much to clean.

Mrs. Kenker uses white linen with china plates and two crystal wine goblets, for she and the mister tip back a few each night. I am keeping an eye on her.

Two days later

Now that Aunt June's feeling better she took her calendar around until she found someone who'd been making notches in the side of a wagon. We think it is May 8, Saturday, 1847.

In the distance there's a light green ribbon stretched through the middle of a wide valley. Pa said this is the Platte River and it will guide us into the mountains. The days are warming up so Pepper and I take our shoes off to walk—this is after we're out of our mothers' sight. The tops of our feet are brown from the sun, the bottoms are tough as leather.

She is more talkative now and not at all shy about lifting her skirt to cool off when no one's looking. I'm fond of her, for she knows how to laugh, and she also has a soft heart. Like me, she's worried about the lost children and their poor mother, more so maybe because she and Wade themselves are twins. We still look behind us, hoping to see dust from their family's wagon trying to catch up.

Wade joined us today with one of his new friends, a tall boy with curly brown hair and a gentle manner. His name is Gideon. He's seventeen years old, but so shy he took one look at Pepper's beautiful green eyes and blushed. He stared down at his feet almost the whole three hours we walked together.

Wade, now, he's not shy. He told a joke when he figured I was the only one listening to him. It went like this: XXXXXXXXXXXXXXXXXXXXX XXXXXXXXXXXXXXXXXXXXXXXXXXXXXX XXXXXXXXXXXXXXXXXXXXXXXXXXXXXX XXXXXXXXXXXXXXXXXXXXXXXXXXXXXX

XXXXXXXXXXXXXXXXXXXXXXXXXXXXXXXXX
XXXXXXXXXXXXXXXXXXXXXXXXXXXXXXXXX
XXXXXXXXXX

(Aunt June saw over my shoulder while I was sitting after supper and said I must not repeat such naughty jokes, and that I best cross it out before Ma sees.)

But I still think it was funny.

May 10, Monday

As we headed down a bluff toward the Platte River there was already many campfires, tents, and wagons. It felt the same as when our steamboat arrived in Independence —so many people!

Most are from Wisconsin Territory — they have "northern" accents, a speech that is not near as slow as folks' from Kentucky. Some brothers from Iowa have brung with them 800 young fruit trees to plant in Oregon. The seedlings are just a few inches tall.

"Well," said Pa, "seems these here are our new traveling companions."

The trail is broad and sandy here on the south side of the Platte, and it feels like we're pulling uphill. Pa says we'll go over one hundred miles before we have to cross, and it'll take maybe ten days.

(I do dread having to cross another river.)

Mosquitoes are fierce! There are itchy bites on my arms, neck, and cheeks, even on my head where my hair is parted. It is near impossible not to scratch vigorously.

Every morning we fry up "skeeter cakes." I've tried and tried to stir quick and even if the batter is clean when I pour, somehow bugs see it as a place to land, and land they do, like specks of pepper. I can see no way around it.

At night there are campfires way across the river, on the north side. Our men are talking low among themselves, wondering if Indians are following us. (If they *are* following us, what are we to do?) Come sunup, all we can see is dust and horses and what looks like wagons, but Pa says if they ain't Indians what are they and why do they travel alone?

Evening

Tall Joe and three of his friends crossed over by way of sandbars and shallows to see who these strangers are.

"They're Mormons, from Illinois," Tall Joe reported back to us. "Their leader is a big fella named Brigham Young. There is only three women and two children and the rest is men, about one hundred forty we counted, and three nigras, servants looks like."

Tall Joe said they're heading west, maybe to the valley of the Great Salt Lake to start a colony. "Thousands more will come next year, don't ask me why, it's just a desert full of dead things."

Pa asked Tall Joe, "But why do they stay on the other side of the river? There ain't no trail."

"I dunno," the old trapper said between mouthfuls of beans. "Maybe they's worried there won't be enough grass, I dunno."

A wagon train is like a small town the way talk spreads. Soon everyone, it seems, had a story about the Mormons, mainly that Mormon men each have several wives and the reason they left

Illinois is because they want to find a place to live where folks won't keep telling them they're committing adultery.

Mrs. Lewis said, "Frankly I prefer they stay on the other side of the river on account of I don't want any pole-igamist getting friendly with our daughters and sisters. Leave ol' Brigham Young be. Let them go their way."

Myself, personally I think something's wrong with a religion that says men get to have as many wives as they please all at once. Pepper says so, too.

Before bed

Forgot to say that today Bennie took off his shirt and threw it in the river. I don't know why he did this except that he's two years old and doesn't know better. Now he has one shirt to last all the way to Oregon. I must watch carefully to make sure he don't also throw away his shoes!

Next day

At noon Mama was looking through our kitchen box, taking things out then putting them back.

"Hattie?" she said. "Have you seen Grandma's china plate, the little one with roses? I thought I put it in after breakfast."

I helped Ma look. We tried to think together where we last set it. Suddenly I caught my breath, remembering:

Pepper and I had carried our families' dishes to the stream where we dipped them in cold water and rubbed them with sand. To dry, we lay them on the grassy bank and sat for a while talking. There were other women doing the same. One of them was Mrs. Kenker.

I'm worried Mrs. Kenker has stole something else from us, but if I tell Ma, there might be arguments and Ma is already wore out and nervous as it is. I don't want to bother her with something new to worry about.

(How can someone who looks like my dear old grandmother be a thief?)

After supper when the fiddlers were getting

warmed up, I walked over to the Kenkers' wagon, just to see what I could see. Mister and Missus were sitting on stools by their wheel, talking sweet to the Anderson family. The five little girls were on a blanket that was laid out in the dirt, playing with a tea set they made from acorn caps. Cassia was singing a song to her baby sister, Eliza May.

"Hello, Hattie, dear," Mrs. Kenker said. "We're having cocoa in a moment, would you like to join us?"

"No, ma'am, I would not." I kept walking.

"My, my," she said.

I know it wasn't polite to answer her so sharp, but I don't care.

Later

We are camped by the Platte. Smoke from the Mormon campfires drifts toward us with a good smell of beef roasting. I would like to meet the two Mormon children and see what they're like, what kind of clothes they're wearing, and so forth. How lonesome it must be for them not to have friends to play with on such a long journey.

Mosquitoes are still a terrible nuisance. Every bit of my skin itches! Ma says the only way to keep them off is to smear mud on our bites, but I tried this three nights in a row. By sunup my face was so tight I couldn't smile and when it was all washed off my skin was dry as a stone, which itched almost as bad as the bites.

Pepper and I followed a tiny stream out of camp to a marshy area. Growing nearby was a small crop of wild carrots and parsnips. We pulled their bushy tops until we had enough to fill our aprons. I dislike vegetables, they make me feel vomitty, but Aunt June says to gather any food we see because we don't know what tomorrow will bring. Along the path we also found a tree with tiny green apples, but left them as they weren't ripe.

Another day

Something horrible has happened and I fear I'm to blame.

Just before supper last night little Cassia came to where Pepper and I was cutting up potatoes and onions for soup. While Cassia watched, I sliced all the parsnips and gave her a couple bites when she held out her palm.

The kettle was hanging over a fire near the center of camp, so Pepper and I brung the vegetables along with three salted ox tongues, preserved from those that died the other day. We dumped the meat and onions into the boiling water, but saved the rest to add later.

We returned to help Mrs. Lewis — Pepper's mother — make pies. I rolled out dough on the wagon seat, enough for six pie crusts. This took near an hour. While I was pressing them into pans, we heard screams.

Lying in the dirt by the kettle was three boys. They were shaking and twisting and foaming at the mouth and gasping for breath. When we saw that one of the boys was Wade, Pepper and her mother ran with their hands in the air crying out his name.

Such was my hurry that when I jumped down from the seat my skirt swept the pie crusts off, down into the dirt.

"What is it? What's happened?" Wade's mother cried, pulling him into her arms. Pa noticed the basket of vegetables had been knocked over.

He scooped up a handful and yelled, "No one eat anything! No one!" He leapt onto a crate so folks could see him, and kept hollering. "Who made this soup? What's in it?"

I was so frightened my insides were shivering, but I stepped forward. Pepper did, too.

"Pa," I said, trying not to cry, "it was our turn to cook tonight, we made it."

"Hattie, show me what you put in, quick." To the gathering men he shouted, "Bury all this, bury it now." Meanwhile some of the women were scooping charcoal from the fire and crushing it into powder. They tried to force it down the boys' throats with water, but their jaws was clenched too tight.

Pepper and I showed Pa where we cut the meat and vegetables. He picked up the potato peelings, smelled them, put a piece on his tongue and waited a moment. He did the same with an onion skin. He tasted a sliver of beef.

"These here are all right," he said. "What else, Hattie?"

I showed him the parsnip tops we'd broke off and set aside for salad.

Pa's face fell. He looked up at Mr. Lewis then back at me. He sniffed the greens, then placed a tiny bit of the root on the tip of his tongue.

In an instant he spit it out. "God help us," he said. "This is water hemlock . . . poison. Hattie, wash your hands right quick."

Next day

It's midmorning and we are still camped.

There is so much upset and noise that I am alone in our wagon for a few moments. No one can see me because I'm hidden among the flour sacks; wish I could disappear for good.

When Pa said the word "hemlock," panic broke out. Folks who hadn't eaten yet suddenly

53

thought they had. Mothers cried for their children. Suddenly I remembered Cassia.

We called her name. Gideon found her curled up inside his family's wagon. When I saw him carrying her limp body in his arms, and when I realized she was dead, I broke down.

"Only two bites," I sobbed. "It was only two bites."

Three graves are being dug by the side of the trail. The two younger boys died thirty minutes after becoming sick. Wade hasn't woke up yet. His eyes just stare, and his body stiffens and shakes so wildly they've had to tie him down so he won't hurt himself. Pepper is too upset to speak.

It crushed me to look at Wade. He is breathing hard and fast through clenched jaws so it sounds like he's hissing. Blood is at the corners of his mouth. I have never seen such a violent sickness.

What happened was the boys were so hungry they sampled the vegetables while waiting for supper.

We don't know how much hemlock Wade ate, but we're praying it ain't as much as the others.

He was the only one whose jaws they were able to pry open long enough for him to swallow. Maybe charcoal in his stomach is absorbing the poison.

There is much weeping.

Pepper and I showed the men where we found the plants. We are showing them to everyone, walking from wagon to wagon, telling children to be careful, to stay away and not even touch them if they find any while out playing.

Pa said at first there is a sweet taste when you take a bite, but then there is a bitter, burning taste. Carrots and parsnips, he showed us by drawing in the dirt, have one root, that's what they are, a root. Hemlock has a few roots joined together, like a hand with plump fingers. The color is white, just like parsnips and wild carrots.

Even the tops are deadly. Sheep and cattle die from grazing on them. Uncle Tim said that one small root can kill a horse, one bite can kill a man.

He showed us that when you cut hemlock it drips with an oily yellow goo. The other thing is the roots are hollow with rungs. Like rungs in a ladder. I'm sick to think I didn't know these things.

Later

We have pulled out and left behind that terrible camp along the Platte. Gideon and Mr. Lewis — Wade's father — carved the children's names onto a plank of wood, along with a warning, and placed it by the graves.

The funeral was unbearable . . . oh, the tears. We stood with Cassia's parents and sisters. The boys' families also had many aunts, uncles, brothers, and cousins. A lone fiddler played "Amazing Grace" as men shoveled dirt onto the common grave. Moments later the sun set, spreading gold and purple across the wide flowing river. I ached something fierce.

Mrs. Anderson looked at me with eyes full of sorrow, then gently brushed my cheek before turning away.

Later, when the stars were out and no one could see me, I ran into the brush and fell down weeping. My heart was broken. Everyone says I'm not to blame, but still I feel dead inside. It's a miracle no one else ate the vegetables.

Wade seems to sleep, but his eyes are open and he mumbles words we don't understand. They gave him a sip of rum this morning which has made his arms and jaw relax. Pepper lifts a spoonful of water to his lips every half hour and rubs her finger along his throat so he'll swallow. He must have bitten his cheek because there is still blood in his mouth.

Our mothers pray. They are asking God, that if it be His will, to please heal Wade.

I look over at the Anderson wagon and start crying again. There are half as many diapers pinned to their canvas top. Ma said there's nothing worse than losing a child. And to leave behind the grave, never to see it again, is an unspeakable pain.

Lord, please don't let Wade die.

I don't know what day this is

We crossed the South Platte. I've not felt like writing until now.

This river is near a mile wide and so shallow lots of folks walk across. This was a very great relief to me.

Pepper and I challenged Gideon and some other boys to a race, but we were soon slowed down by our wet skirts. When Gideon saw us struggling to run in the waist-high water, he stepped between us, took our hands, and helped pull us across.

It was the first time any of us had laughed for two days.

Once ashore we flopped down in the warm sand and stared up at the sky. It was such a lovely blue, I felt, for that moment, happy again.

While Pepper and I wrung out our hems, Gideon turned away, embarrassed to see our bare legs. He is the nicest of all the boys we've met except for Wade. I feel sad Wade's been sleeping these two days. His mama keeps a damp cloth over his eyes so he won't go blind.

Later

Now that we're in the North Platte River Valley the air feels dry and thin. My lips are so chapped they bleed when I talk. The only thing to do is dip our fingers into the bucket of axle grease and rub our lips every hour or so. It smells bad, it tastes bad, and the blowing dust sticks.

It feels like we must be halfway to Oregon, but Tall Joe says, no, we've only gone five hundred miles. He also said the worst part of the trail is to come.

Does he mean more rivers to cross? Will there be Indians? I'm afraid to ask what he's talking about.

The Andersons' wagon had an accident when we climbed up Windlass Hill and were heading down the other side. It was so steep that at the top of the hill we unhitched the teams and led them down separately. Then we chained the wheels to keep them from turning.

Also we cut small trees and tied them behind each wagon for drag, to slow it down as men lowered them with ropes and pulleys. (That's why this place is named Windlass Hill.)

It took hours and hours. I was nervous watching the men strain so hard, their heels dug into sand, their palms bleeding from the ropes. Ma and some other ladies tore their petticoats into rags to wrap around the men's hands.

What happened with the Anderson wagon is that their front axle hit a stump which caused the smaller rope to snap. Before anyone could help, the wagon flipped over and over and over, landing in splinters at the bottom. Folks screamed, but it was just the shock of seeing such an accident. No one was hurt. Thank God Mrs. Anderson and her daughters were watching from the top of the hill, for they had climbed out earlier to lighten the load.

The only belongings they could rescue were clothes and blankets that were strewn over the rocks when their trunks split open, and a few tools. Aunt June and Uncle Tim right away invited the family to share their own wagon and supplies for the rest of the journey.

We also will share. Hazel, Holly, Laurel, and Olive will take turns riding with us. I don't mind giving up my very small spot inside as it's hot from the sun beating down on the canvas top. I am tired of the bumping and rattling, besides something always tips over, yesterday it was Ma's bureau. Things are packed in so tight that the bouncing makes the ropes fray. (My opinion is it ain't safe in there.)

Two other wagons got "stumped" today, so those families will double up with others. There's enough wreckage to completely build a new rig, but no time to do it. We must keep moving. The mules and oxen will go to others who need them.

After supper Gideon came over to where Pepper and I were sitting. He nodded to me then looked shyly at Pepper. "Woncha please dance with me?" he asked.

Pepper leaned over to whisper in my ear. "Do you mind, Hattie?"

I turned to whisper in her ear, "He's handsome!"

She smiled, then squeezed my hand. So there they are, circling the fire with other dancers, shuffling, stepping, turning—his left hand on his hip, his right hand around her waist. Folks watch them and smile.

I wish Wade was well enough to ask me to dance.

Ash Hollow

The Platte split into two, so now our trail is along the North Platte River. Our reward for making it down Windlass Hill is the most beautiful campsite yet. It's called Ash Hollow because of so many thick, shady ash trees.

There's a spring with fresh icy water so we can fill up our barrels and such. Everywhere we look there's firewood and good pasture for the animals. It is so peaceful Ma said, "Oh, Charles, can't we stay here forever?"

A few years ago some emigrants did exactly that. A family built themselves a cabin and plowed a field. They are friendly to us and have offered to post our letters with the next travelers heading back to Missoura. Many of us quick wrote to friends. I tore out a sheet of paper from this journal and sent Becky a drawing of hemlock, telling her all.

The moon is full so I'm writing by its light as I sit near the wagon. There are hundreds of campfires tonight, and singing. Ma is walking along a creek with Mrs. Anderson, who has been silent for days. Ma says she's grieving, that she finally realizes little Cassia is gone and that her grave is far away, in a lonely place along a river she'll never see again.

I'm so very sad for her. This makes me watch Bennie and Jake more close for I don't know how Ma and Pa and me could go on if they became lost or died somehow.

There are Indians, about twenty, camped nearby. The sight of them makes me so nervous I feel vomitty.

Some women came near, holding their hands out, talking in their language. Their deerskin dresses have tiny beads sewn along their sleeves. Their hair is braided over their shoulders. One of them wore a basket on her back with a baby inside, a dark-haired baby with dark quiet eyes. They accepted Ma's corncakes without a smile.

I asked Tall Joe why they was begging. "They ain't begging," he said. "Indians are hospitable people and if they was passing through our land they'd give us a gift. They're just asking for ours."

They look like beggars to me, but they are not making trouble. Matter of fact one of the women did something real nice. She saw Mrs. Anderson off by herself, crying, and walked over to her with a square of deerskin, the size of a plate. On it was several chunks of cooked meat.

She picked up a piece and put it to Mrs. Anderson's lips, nodding for her to eat. The woman then pointed to the little Anderson girls playing in the stream, then motioned with her hands and mouth, like she was eating.

Finally Mrs. Anderson accepted the gift. I think she understood that the Indian woman wanted her to take nourishment for the sake of her little daughters.

Later

Aunt June wears a smock dress now on account she's getting bigger. I helped her and Ma do laundry. The stream was busy with ladies talking and working. By afternoon the bushes were covered with petticoats, shirts, calicoes, blankets — all drying in the hot sun.

The youngest children ran naked into the water. Pepper and I loosened our braids and stripped down to our camisoles then jumped in, too. How good the cold water felt pouring over my face and through my hair, and how good it felt to wash away the dust.

We swam downstream along the bank where willows made a canopy of shade. It was shallow enough to sit on the sandy bottom, the water up to our shoulders. Ma don't know this, but we then took off our drawers and camisoles until we was bare as the day we were born. Reckless with joy, we dove below the surface to stare at each other through the bubbles.

It was several minutes before we realized our clothes was floating downstream far beyond our reach, down in the direction of the men and boys.

Pepper and I soon learned it ain't easy to walk upstream crouched down so only your head is above water. Also, it is near impossible to swim without your bare backside showing.

We was rescued by two grandmothers holding blankets for us.

There is dancing again tonight (Ma still refuses to join in). Pepper was fetched by Gideon and this time he held her hand all the way through camp.

Oh, yes, a little baby girl was born this morning at Ash Hollow.

Another thing, that fat lady came over and brung Ma a fresh pie, mince it turns out. I hurried off to watch from the trees. She must eat ten pies a day, I reckon; she's that huge.

Next day

In the far distance the prairie and low hills are black. I thought there must have been a fire, but

Tall Joe said, "Nope, it's just buffalo, thousands and thousands of 'em."

After supper I sat by the fire to mend Bennie's blanket. He lay next to me in the dirt, talking about this and that, then suddenly he was fast asleep. I like the way he folds into my arms when I carry him to bed.

Later

We are starting to find buffalo droppings, and Tall Joe says, "Where there's buffs, there's Injuns."

Hunters leave the wagons every morning to look for game. They brung down two buffalo near enough to the trail so folks can see them being skinned and butchered. Jake went with some older boys to watch but I stayed behind.

Aunt June was resting in her wagon with Olive and Laurel, who are three and four years old. To make room inside, Uncle Tim pulled out several sacks of bacon and flour.

(It is so much work to pack and unpack that

at noon Pa just lies flat in the dirt to rest and he's sound asleep before his eyes even close.)

We're camped next door to Aunt June with a tarp stretched between the tops for shade. I saw Mrs. Kenker wave howdee.

"Hattie dear," she said, "may I borrow one of your mother's tablecloths please? Mine is soiled and Mr. Kenker is ready for his lunch."

I felt stiff toward her. "I'm afraid not, Mrs. Kenker."

My aunt's voice came from her wagon. "Hattie Campbell, we are not a family to refuse hospitality. Help Mrs. Kenker take what she needs."

Well. By the time Mrs. Kenker had snooped around, we were quite a bit lighter. She took our lovely lace tablecloth that Grandmother made, five doilies, a tea cozy, and one English teacup. She also grabbed one of Ma's brown calico skirts and draped it over her arm, but I snatched it back.

Our eyes locked, then finally she turned away. "Thank you, dear," she called over her shoulder, her arms too full to wave.

Jake was so excited to tell about the buffalo

skinning and he pulled my hand to go see, but I was bothered about Mrs. Kenker and wouldn't.

When Ma came back I told her, but she said the same thing as Aunt June: "We must share."

This makes me mad. I like to share with nice folks, not those that takes advantage. I'm afraid if I say anything more about Mrs. Kenker I'll sound wretched, so that's all for now.

Later again

There are more and more buffalo. They are so many, the herds look like a dark stain moving over the hills. The droppings are flat, full of dried grass and make good coals, but it takes near a bushel to make a decent cooking fire.

I would rather pick up twigs and logs than buffalo dung, but this is what we must do. As long as they're not fresh and gooey, it ain't so bad.

The boys, including my naughty brother Jake, spend much of their chore time throwing these buffalo chips at each other, like a snowball fight, instead of helping. They also think it's fun to ambush us girls, but I think it's nasty.

Pepper and I feel nervous when we go out to gather the chips. The other day two horsemen were watching from a distance, so we told our fathers who told the rest of the men. Now they all ride with loaded guns. It scares me to think Indians are following us.

Maybe Indian women are nice, but the men carry weapons. I do not trust them.

I walk alongside Wade's wagon with Pepper. She and I sing to him "Yankee Doodle" and other songs. We feel silly, but maybe he'll wake up. He's swallowing the broth she spoons into his mouth and his arms no longer shake or stiffen. Mrs. Lewis and her friends look in on him constantly and I will say he's the most prayed-over boy I ever met.

Evening

The sun is scorching hot. Ma insists I wear my bonnet to protect my face, but the cloth itches my scalp. When Pepper and I are out walking we carry them like baskets to gather flowers. It feels cooler to let the wind blow my hair back and besides, I think boys like looking at us better without them.

The Mormons are still on the north side of the Platte. Sometimes all we see is their dust because they move faster. Ma says it's because they're traveling with just two children instead of 200, like we have in our train; babies slow things up—that's just the way it is, she says.

I told Pa that Brigham Young must be very religious because he makes his people rest on the Sabbath—no traveling.

Pa laughed. He said, "I still ain't in agreement with Brigham Young's theology but if he wants to rest on the Sabbath good for him. But, Hattie, don't judge a man only by how strict he keeps rules."

Tall Joe said that up here soon the routes will meet at Fort Laramie and, like it or not, we'll be traveling alongside the Mormons and their 73 wagons. Pepper and I plan to meet the two children.

Later

There is much celebration today and tears of joy.

After three days of sleeping, Wade sat up, looked around and said, "Mother, I am hungry as a bear." Just like that.

Pepper and I joined hands with Gideon and the little Anderson girls and Jake and Bennie. We danced around Wade's wagon and sang. Mrs. Lewis cries and cries she is so thankful to God for healing her son.

He is too weak to walk, but his father carried him down to the river's edge, to a sandy beach. He bathed him then helped him dress into clean clothes. Now Wade's sitting in the shade, wearing a blue shirt and pants.

I am so glad to see his beautiful green eyes again. Pepper can't stop giggling she's so happy. She sits by her brother just talking and talking to him.

Another day

Clouds build up like white towers, then in the afternoon they turn black. Near every day we hear the low rumblings of thunder, and we feel heavy drops of rain — enough to settle the dust and coat the wheels with mud, but no downpour.

We see mighty herds of buffalo in the distance, to either side of the trail. Often there are men on horseback moving along a ridge. If Indians are following us, they're keeping their distance.

Maybe they are just curious and don't plan to murder us.

This morning I read back through this journal and laughed when I saw what I'd written about Booneville: ". . . I am afraid of only four things . . ."

Ma says that people who are thinkers often change their opinions. It means you're growing. So here's what I think.

Some things I was afraid of I'm not afraid of now and the other way around. I am not so scared about snakes anymore, I have not had a toothache, and the Indians haven't hurt us. Even Bennie and Jake don't worry me so much, they are much stronger on their legs and stay close to the wagon. So here is my new list.

1. I'm afraid of hemlock
2. fast rivers

That's all!

Later

Wade walked today, for about fifteen minutes. He steps slow and gets tired easy. When we ask if he remembers what happened he squints and looks up at the sky.

"Nope," he says after a while. He knows we're on our way to Oregon and he does remember being on a riverboat some time ago. He knows his family and today he said my name.

He said, "Hattie, your cheeks are sunburned." Then he smiled at me.

At noon we sat by a stream where it was shady. Aunt June and Mrs. Anderson have become close friends and the four girls are like having my very own sisters again. Ma helps care for baby Eliza

May. We were cooling our feet in the water when we heard loud voices arguing.

Two men were yelling words I can't repeat. I ran through the grass and saw Mr. Kenker with a pistol pointed at Tall Joe and there was Mrs. Kenker, her hands on her hips, also yelling.

Tall Joe yanked off his beaver hat and threw it to the dirt. "Fifteen miles a day is what we'll do like it or not," he said, his face two inches away from Mr. Kenker's. Spit came out he was so mad. "And the next time you point a gun at me, mister, I'll slice your ears off—don't you forget."

Mrs. Kenker piped in. "How dare you speak to my husband that way, we're just poor old people looking to start a new life and you're nothing but a liar who stinks to high heaven. I don't know why we ever let you be the leader."

Tall Joe's eyes narrowed. "And you," he said, pointing his finger at her, "you bother me worse than a corpse on a hot day." He grabbed Mr. Kenker's pistol and aimed it at their wagon seat where a pie was cooling. The first shot made the pan spin, the second splattered it.

Mrs. Kenker's hands flew up in shock and what she screamed at Tall Joe, I ain't repeating that either.

Pa later told us that the Kenkers have been pestering Tall Joe to slow down because they are plumb wore out. The mister has something wrong with his backside so it hurts him to sit so many hours driving their team and she don't like the bugle at 4 o'clock every morning and there's too many crying children and so on, one complaint after another.

I was upset to see old people yelled at, they must be 50 years of age. Even though I don't trust Mrs. Kenker she sometimes still reminds me of my grandmother, the way she looks I mean.

Last week in May, thereabouts

In the far distance we can see something poking up from the horizon like a thumb pointing at the clouds. Tall Joe says this is Chimney Rock. It is the closest thing to a mountain that I have ever seen.

The woman who had a baby back in Ash Hollow died of fever this morning. She was buried on a bluff overlooking the valley. Her newborn daughter is being cared for by another mother, and friends are helping the father with his three little boys.

Chimney Rock

For two long days we approached Chimney Rock . . . it seemed to take forever. Two evenings we watched the sun set behind it as we ate supper.

Now that we're here it's a curious sight, a huge pile of rocks with what looks like a stone chimney rising up from its center. Jake and several boys hiked around its base and counted ten thousand steps. I don't know how they kept track of so many numbers, but they did. Tall Joe said some other folks counted years past and they also said ten thousand.

Boys with rifles are shooting at the top of Chimney Rock to see what will happen. They like the fuss and noise. Now some families have souvenir chips tucked in their wagons.

The plains are dry with no trees. We are slowly moving toward the Pacific Ocean, but it's near impossible for me to picture a sea other than this sea of grass. All around is open space with colors of gold, green, and brown. I feel we are specks, like bugs crawling across a kitchen floor.

It is very pretty, but I miss the sight and smell of trees and I do miss my Missoura River. To think I might never again hear the long, high whistle of a steamboat makes me feel lonesome.

Scott's Bluff

I have never seen a real castle, but today we passed what Pa says looks like one. On the side of the trail, high above us, rose a sharp wall of stone called Scott's Bluff. Jake wanted to climb it when he saw some older boys trying, but Ma held his shirt and said, "No."

The bluff hugs the river so close we had to steer the wagons aside and pull around it, up a rocky ridge. Tall Joe said this place was named after the fur trader Hiram Scott who got sick and was abandoned by his companions. He crawled sixty miles trying to find them. When the trappers came this way again they found his skeleton and what was left of his boots right here.

This morning after we were on the trail for an hour, a boy playing with his father's gun accidentally shot our front ox in the head. It dropped dead so quick the ones behind stumbled onto it and what a tangle of hooves and harnesses. Pa was so mad he stormed over to the boy, grabbed the gun, and threw it into the river.

"You coulda killed one of my children, young man."

I have never seen Pa so red in the face.

I ran to Jake and Bennie, even though I knew they was safe, and gathered them to me like I was an old hen. That boy made me so mad that after supper I marched over and kicked him hard in the leg. Twice.

Sixty miles until we reach Fort Laramie, four days if we push.

Later

Thunder and lightning with heavy winds. Rain turned to sleet then hail. I scolded Jake for throwing hailstones at another boy who ran to his mama crying.

Fort Laramie

When Fort Laramie drew into sight I felt shaky. Indians were camped everywhere! But I looked at them careful and did not see any trouble brewing. They was mostly families, seemed like.

Tall Joe said we're now in the middle of Sioux country and this is the biggest trading post around. It's built from logs and is owned by the American Fur Company. There are dozens of trappers and mountain men dressed in beaded leather and skins and living in tipis. Many seem to be married to Indian women for there are half-breed children playing among the tents.

We're staying for two nights and one full day so folks can make repairs on wagons and buy supplies. A Frenchman runs this place.

Way on the other side of the river we can see Brigham Young's camp. The trail, such as it is, ends so they must cross to our side. The Frenchman has a flatboat. For fifteen dollars he'll ferry their wagons across. Fifteen dollars is a fortune, but Pa says the river is deeper here so it's probably worth it for them to pay.

We were already on the trail again before the Mormons had crossed over, so I reckon they'll be traveling in our dust.

There are signposts every few miles. These are messages written on pieces of board stuck in the sand, also there are buffalo skulls with writing on them. Some notes are impossible to read because the sun has bleached out the ink, or rain has smeared it. There are warnings of bad water, rattlesnakes, and danger, like this one: "Willie Henderson and two others died here June 1846, buffalo stampede . . ."

Early June

Aunt June feels poorly. Ma says it is just weariness. She needs to rest and to drink more water. I asked when her baby will be born because she walks slower and her middle is bigger by the day it seems.

"Soon, Hattie, in a few weeks."

Mr. Lewis's mules are gone. Sometime in the night they were stolen from their pickets, their ropes cut.

"Injuns," he said, shaking his head with worry. We gave him one of our oxen, now we have four. Uncle Tim did also, so now Mr. Lewis has a team of two.

The Mormons passed us today while we were nooning. Tall Joe pointed out Brigham Young on horseback. He was wearing a black hat and he lifted his arm to wave, then galloped ahead. Pepper and I stood on our wagon seat and shaded our eyes, hoping to see the Mormon children, but we saw only dust.

Someone said that just one wife is with him, all the others are back in Illinois.

Register Cliff

The trail goes through limestone which is soft when wet. Pepper and I carved our names into a boulder by the side of the road using a sharp stone. Our hands grew tired, so we didn't spell out our full names or hometowns.

During the long, hot hours of the day, many of the men driving wagons doze, their reins in hand. It's a wonder none have fallen off the seats. Pa looks wore out. Yesterday a wasp stung him on his neck and it has swollen up. Ma keeps dabbing mud on, but it is still sore and red.

We are so tired by nightfall, we roll into our blankets and stretch out on the hard ground, lately not using tents. It means one less thing to unpack and repack every day.

The breeze is cool on my face. How I wish I could keep my eyes open long enough to study the stars, but suddenly it is morning. The bugle has sounded and campfires smell of fresh coffee.

Afternoon

Pepper told me a secret last night.

We were setting up a tent to share with little Holly and Laurel, for there was thunder and the smell of rain. It was pitch-black, no moon or stars. Every minute or so a sheet of lightning flashed in the west, so bright we could see the whole prairie, the way it is when someone holds up a lantern in a barn. For two full seconds we could see each other, then it was dark again.

After we tucked ourselves into blankets, Holly and Laurel already asleep between us, Pepper whispered.

"Gideon has asked me to marry him . . . and I said yes. Tell me what you think, Hattie."

"Well, Pepper, I'm real happy for you."

But what I didn't tell her was that I was filled with envy. How I wanted to have someone love me, too. If she is fourteen and old enough to marry, then I at thirteen am old enough to fall in love.

We whispered until the rain began hitting our tent and we could no longer hear one another.

It rained all night. Pepper and I moved closer

and held the little girls against us so they wouldn't be cold. Thunder rocked the ground as if horses were running by.

Water seeped under our tent and up into our blankets. I did not sleep a wink on account of being wet and chilled.

Next day

Wet blankets were hung to dry inside the wagons and outside, pinned to the canvas. They soon were so full of trail dust that it was a chore to shake the mud loose. Tall Joe says last night was just a dribble, nothing compared to the heavy rains he's seen in years past, so we should shut up and count ourselves lucky.

When word spread that Gideon and Pepper planned to marry, the women began putting together a wedding chest for them. Aunt June emptied one of her trunks and began folding and packing gifts that folks brought.

A beautiful down quilt came from one family. There was bedsheets and linens, a tarp, lantern, and dutch oven, an axe and a kettle. I gave her my tin of Babbitt's powdered soap. One lady brought over her own lace nightgown and petticoat, never worn, that she'd been saving to wear once she got to Oregon.

"May as well have a bride enjoy them now," she said. "Oregon is a long way off and who knows what'll happen between now and then."

Pepper and Gideon take long walks in the evening, then appear in time for the last dance. They hold hands until the fire is low. She's late crawling into our bed and I wake up to her whispering in my ear, "Hattie?"

For a while we watch the stars and talk and wonder about the mysteries of marriage. But I worry, will she still be my friend? Will we live next door to each other like we planned?

Later

I am ashamed of myself.

Today the fat lady came over to visit, but Ma was down by the creek. I was figuring on how to act busy when the lady said, "Hello, honey. I've made some taffy for you to share with your brothers. Here you go."

She handed me the candy wrapped in oilcloth and smiled at me so kindly I felt ashamed that I had avoided her so. Right quick I invited her to tea, recollecting Aunt June having told me to be hospitable.

While the kettle was set over the fire to boil the lady went to her wagon and came back with her husband riding on her wide shoulders. They introduced themselves as Mr. and Mrs. Bigg. (Cross my heart I did not laugh at their name.)

Mrs. Bigg said she has to drive the wagon on account of her husband being crippled. He sits next to her to keep her company and now I recall seeing them talk and laugh together hour after hour, like old friends. Because he has no legs and the trail is so rough, he ties himself to the bench so he won't bounce off.

They said that a few years ago he was trampled by horses from a runaway wagon and his crushed legs had to be amputated. Poor man. I've decided they are two of the nicest folks I ever did meet and I will strike anyone who makes fun of them or the fact that her name describes her.

(I am so glad I kept my first opinions to myself! If Pepper knew how unkind I can be, I would melt from shame.)

Later

When Mrs. Bigg heard that Pepper is to be married, she dug in her trunk and pulled out one of her lace tablecloths. She marched over to our camp pulling a cart where Mr. Bigg sits like he's riding in a little train. She held the lace up to Pepper and said, "Honey, I'm gonna make you the prettiest wedding dress you'll ever set eyes on."

And she did.

For five evenings Mrs. Bigg sewed and cut and measured until she had a creamy white dress with long sleeves and a bow that ties at the waist. Mr. Bigg sat beside her in his cart, sewing, too. He made a lacy overskirt from curtains that had hung in their parlor back in Missoura.

Finally we gathered by her wagon and held up blankets to make a private room. Pepper carefully stepped into the dress. As her mother buttoned up the back, the ladies caught their breaths she looked so beautiful.

The wedding is planned for when we arrive at Independence Rock, a few days away.

A hot afternoon

Mrs. Anderson came over this morning as we were packing up our breakfast plates. She looks very thin, but there's more color to her cheeks. I can hardly look at her without wanting to cry for little Cassia.

She said to Ma, "It was so warm last night I think I left my shawl by your fire. Have you seen it, Augusta?"

Together they looked under the wagon, by the crates and stools, then in Aunt June's wagon. I remember it was a pretty blue shawl with fringe. We looked and looked.

Wade is feeling good enough to dance, but

when the fiddlers started up he asked another girl! I was so upset I ran outside the circle where it was dark. For a long time I sat in the dirt where no one could see me, watching the dancers. I felt so alone.

I want someone to love me the way Gideon loves Pepper.

Mid-June

The North Platte River runs west, but now we've come to where it makes a sharp turn to the south. We must cross it in order to continue toward Oregon.

Imagine our surprise to see that the Mormons not only had come and gone, but left behind nine men to build a ferry. Two ferries. And they would be glad to help us get across for just a dollar fifty per wagon.

My, the arguments that broke out because of this. Tall Joe said that over his dead body would he pay one penny to cross a river that he saw years before Brigham Young even knew it existed.

But Pa said, "I think it's mighty enterprising of the Mormons to start a business in such a faraway place."

Mr. and Mrs. Kenker cursed something fierce thinking they might need to part with some of their money. Several families said this: "Those Mormons are so high and mighty they stayed on the other side of the river and wouldn't associate with us. But now that they can make a dollar off us they're friendly as can be."

"Come on, folks," Pa said. "Brigham Young's people are trying to start a new life, just like us. And I'll tell you something else . . . we ain't their judge, God Almighty is, so let's get going and not be so mad about everything."

He and Uncle Tim bargained with the Mormons. Two sacks of cornmeal paid our passage across, on rafts made from thin logs and strips of leather. Each raft, they said, could hold up to 1,800 pounds, but I don't know.

It felt unsteady, and water washed over my feet as I helped Ma hold the wagon. I was so scared we'd sink, my knees ached from standing stiff.

The littlest children sat safe inside, real still so the wagon wouldn't rock.

Pa and Uncle Tim swam with the animals, my little brother Jake on the back of a mule. The water came up to his waist, but his fingers were hooked tight into the harness. I kept an eye on him, ready to dive in if he should slip off.

Once our family and the Andersons were all safe across that deep river, I was not so nervous.

It took six days to get everyone over. Many refused to pay the Mormons and instead forded the river without help. Except for wet belongings and scared children everything was all right until the last day, when we heard screams.

I looked out and there in the middle of the current was two wagons side by side, their mules swimming hard, their big brown heads straining for breath. Somehow one of the mules drifted downstream into the other team and got its hooves tangled in the harnesses.

That poor mule panicked, then right before our eyes the animals began to drown. They sank so fast they pulled the wagons underwater before anyone had a chance to jump out. Two families disappeared just like that. I am sick at heart. The screams of their friends on shore I will never ever forget as long as I live.

For one day the men searched for bodies while the last of the families came over. Meanwhile everyone stayed busy doing regular things, almost like nothing bad had happened.

Pa said the nine Mormons will take apart their wagons to build a cabin, then stay till more pioneers come out next summer.

This gave Pa and Mr. Lewis an idea.

Soon enough they had bartered wood to make a small wagon with three hoops. They bought a tent, and with the help of Mr. and Mrs. Bigg's sewing, turned the canvas into a top. They traded beans for two mules with harnesses and neck collars.

"What on earth?" asked Ma. There stood a miniature prairie schooner, about five feet long and three feet wide, with one set of wheels.

Mr. Lewis grinned when he answered, "It's a wedding gift for my daughter and Gideon."

Pa made friends with one of the Mormons, a man named Appleton M. Harmon, and they got to talking about something Brigham Young and his men invented on the trail to measure miles. It's called a "road-o-meter." He drew Pa a picture in the sand and it looks like four or five wooden cogs attached to a wagon wheel. Somehow it works.

The Mormons also have something like a thermometer that measures "barometric pressure." This is how they know the altitude.

Later

We are camped at the Sweetwater River. I watched from shore while my brothers played in the shallows with some other children. The current is slow but still I worry they'll be swept away.

Independence Rock

From a distance this sloped rock looks like a bear sleeping on its side. Up close, it's huge and easy to climb. Folks have been going up to the top to see the view and carve their names. Some boys raced each other up, then fired pistols in the air to celebrate. Jake asked Pa if he could have a few sticks of dynamite to throw off the top, just to see what would happen.

Pa thought a moment. When he said yes, Jake let out a happy yell.

Pepper and I were at the river when we heard the explosion. We turned in time to see a puff of smoke floating down from the top. Some cattle took off running in fright, but were rounded up quick by men on horseback.

I don't understand why boys like such things or why Pa thinks dynamite is safer than rifles.

The wedding was late afternoon, in the cool shadow of Independence Rock. Pepper was beautiful. She was barefoot with a wreath of wildflowers in her hair, and her dress seemed to float with the breeze. Gideon was so shy that when someone yelled, "Kiss the bride!" he blushed redder than a sunburn and just kept holding her hand.

Soon enough there was music and dancing

and food, plenty of it. Wade came up to me smiling, but instead of asking me to dance, he said, "Hattie, wanna play a trick on my sister?"

He led me to their new wagon. Mrs. Lewis and the ladies had made up a cozy bed with curtains for privacy, and there was a lantern hanging from one of the hoops inside. Wade opened a sack that he had brung over earlier, and began pulling out pots, pans, and other trinkets, which he tied with string under the wagon.

I brushed at my apron, nervous. Darkness had fallen. Soon we saw Gideon holding Pepper's hand and leading her away from the campfire. Wade and I ran into the shadows.

When the newlyweds climbed into their wagon, Wade whispered, "Get ready, Hattie." He gave a little whistle and, to my surprise, out of the darkness appeared dozens of men and women, some children, too. All waited for about five minutes, real quiet.

Finally Wade whistled softly. Two men hurried to the front of the wagon, lifted the tongue, and began running as if they was mules. Noise erupted from the pans clanging underneath. The crowd that had gathered ran alongside, whooping and yelling and banging spoons, making the wildest noise I'd ever heard.

We followed the wagon until the men halted at the edge of the prairie, about a mile from camp. The noise stopped. For a moment we heard the perfect quiet of night: crickets and wind sighing through the grass. Then Wade began singing a hymn, in a beautiful slow voice: ". . . May our good Lord watch over you always . . ." After the first verse, everyone joined in, then slowly began walking back to camp where there was still music.

Wade caught up to me. In the firelight I could see his green eyes and he was smiling. "That shivaree was some fun, wasn't it, Hattie?"

Now I was the one to feel shy. Before I could think of something to say, he took my hand and led me past the fiddler to join the other dancers.

Another day

About the Sweetwater River: Tall Joe says it got its name from some trappers who tried to get their mules across during a storm. One of the packs was full of sugar and when its saddle broke, in went 300 pounds of sugar.

Rocks on either side rise up about 400 feet, forming a narrow river canyon called Devil's Gate. The trail drops into nothing so the wagons had to drive on the outside, about half a mile away. It took all day.

Some of us climbed to the top of the cliff for a view. It was spectacular, but it made my stomach turn to look over the ledge, the river was so far down. Tall Joe told us that a few years ago a young bride fell to her death doing what we'd just done.

Another day

My little brother Ben fell off the wagon seat just before noon as we were pulling to a stop. The wheels rolled over his left arm so that it hung like a broken stick. He cried and cried, while Pa set it in a splint.

I ran among the families to look for brandy or rum or something to help his pain. I knocked at the Kenkers' wagon and leaned in. Mrs. Kenker sat on a quilt knitting, her husband asleep beside her.

When I told her about Bennie she said, "Oh my word, how terribly dreadful," and set down her needles. She uncorked a jug and poured whiskey into a tin cup, about two inches deep. "Give this to your brother, dear, and he'll not feel a thing."

I thanked her and hurried back to Ma, trying not to spill the whiskey. Soon Bennie was quiet and as Pa rocked him to sleep I remembered Mrs. Kenker's knitting. Her yarn was the same color blue as Mrs. Anderson's shawl that disappeared.

I'm sure we have a thief among us and worried that I'm the only one who knows. I don't want to bother Pepper about it, and Aunt June is so tired. Ma probably won't believe me on account she says we must always respect our elders no matter what. Grandmothers don't steal, is probably what she'd say.

My cheeks and the back of my hands are peeling from sunburn. I rub in axle grease, but dust sticks to my skin. It is tiresome to feel dirty all the time.

Later

Six oxen died yesterday and one mule. After butchering them where they fell, we kept going. They're too heavy to move and there ain't time to bury them.

Tall Joe made an announcement at supper: We must lighten our loads to make it easier on the tired animals.

Ma said to me, "The dresser and rocker can go, but I will never part with your sisters' things."

When we pulled out this morning there was an odd assortment left in camp: a washtub, an oval mirror, two trunks filled with brand-new shoes, a piano, and a birdcage.

Someone had put several dozen books onto the shelves of a china hutch, neat and tidy as a library.

Maybe folks coming behind will get to enjoy them, but who has time to read?

Tall Joe caught Mrs. Kenker picking through the items and said, "Madam, if your oxen drop dead from all the junk you're making them pull, why, I ain't waiting for you or that husband of yours to find a new team."

The trail seems to be uphill. Today it was our turn to be in front and I thought, at last, we'll have no dust. But the wind was at our backs, so we walked in blowing dirt all day long. My skirt pressed behind my legs, often tripping me.

Jake and I take turns riding in the wagon to help Ma. I don't like it one bit because it is so hot inside—stuffy and cramped—but we must keep Ben still so his arm will heal. Pa said it was a blessing the bone didn't poke through his skin, else they might have had to amputate on account of infection.

Poor Bennie. He wants to play and run alongside the oxen, but Ma is too scared. A boy in one of the other wagons — we don't know the family — was riding on their sideboard. No one knows what happened, but somehow he fell and was trampled by the mules behind. There was so much dust that it wasn't until three wagons passed did they find him.

We all stopped for an hour. They buried him in the middle of the road so wolves won't dig him up. We can hear the boy's mother and sisters wailing, even above the noise of our moving wagons.

Along the Sweetwater

Today when I saw Pepper and Gideon's little wagon she waved me over. "Please walk with me, Hattie," she called.

I was so happy to be with her again. As Gideon drives and she walks alongside, they keep smiling at each other. She is more talkative than ever, which makes me feel good. I think she is glad we are friends.

The next miles of trail twisted through ravines and sandy slopes. We were nervous to see rattlesnakes everywhere, draped over rocks and coiled in the hot sun. Pa said the West is home to these snakes so we must just learn to be careful, is all.

Way ahead in the distance we can see dust from the Mormons. They're at least one day away.

Mosquitoes are terrible and now there're also biting flies. My arms are covered with welts that bleed because I can't help scratching. My sleeves have bloodstains such that I want to rip away the cloth they look so soiled. I wish I had many, many clean dresses instead of this old ragged thing. I yearn to feel pretty again.

Funny, but now I do wear my bonnet and Pepper wears hers. I tease her about being an old married lady but the truth is our faces hurt from sunburn and the skin keeps peeling. The ridge of my nose is so raw it stings. Every night I rub axle grease on it and my lips, too, not hardly minding the stink of it anymore.

There was another wedding last evening. The bride is also fourteen and her new husband about thirty years old. He is a carpenter, the one whose wife died a few weeks ago, before we reached Chimney Rock. So now this girl is a mother of three young sons and a newborn daughter. Some older women are helping her care for the baby and one is nursing it every few hours.

I feel sorry for the girl, all at once having to learn how to be a wife and a mother of four children.

But Ma says things will probably turn out all right because the bride and groom need each other. He was a widower and she was an orphan traveling with an elderly cousin. "They'll grow to love one another, Hattie."

South Pass

Tall Joe says we've come near 900 miles — that means we're almost halfway to Oregon! There are cheers and singing and gunshots.

Pa thought crossing the Continental Divide would be treacherous, but the gap here is twelve miles wide and gentle as a cornfield. The slope is so gradual we hardly knew where we were. To the north are the Wind River Mountains covered with snow. There is a carpet of yellow and blue wildflowers spread between boulders and pine trees, so beautiful. It's sunny, but the air is thin and cold because of the elevation, about 8,000 feet.

Women and girls are picking bouquets to hang upside down in our wagons, so they'll keep their color while drying — this way we'll have flowers during our winter in Oregon.

Tall Joe says the nights are so cold at South Pass we must keep going, down the western slope to a campground called Pacific Creek.

End of June
Pacific Creek

We're camped here for two days to rest and celebrate. It's a wondrous feeling to think we are finally in the West. Now the rivers and streams flow to the Pacific Ocean instead of eastward toward the Atlantic.

Everyone who was able dipped a cup in the water and held it up for a cheer. The fiddlers got busy and soon everyone was ready to dance. Everyone except Mama. She said not until her feet are in Oregon City will she celebrate. (Some moments Mama is so grouchy I know for certain I mustn't upset her with news about our thief.)

For part of the day we shared a campsite with the Mormons. Pepper, Gideon, Wade, and I walked over to their wagons, curious. There was a fire where a spit held a roasting side of beef.

We saw three women busy carrying plates back and forth, but didn't see any children. (I wondered which one was Brigham Young's wife.) A colored man came over and introduced himself by the odd name of Green Flake, then asked us to please leave on account of his people resting.

Someone said he once was a slave, but now is Brigham Young's personal servant.

Sandy Creek

Here the trail splits. Tall Joe said there's a short-cut heading north that'll save seven days. But it's 50 miles of desert, no trees, no water or grass for the animals. The days are blistering hot. The only time to travel is after sundown, when it's cooler.

Or, he said, the safest is to swing southwest down to Fort Bridger. It'll take longer, but it skirts the Wyoming desert.

Our family had a discussion. Pa agreed we'd go with Tall Joe, the safest way, on account of Aunt June might have her baby any day now. Both Ma and Mrs. Anderson begged for the safe route — they're afraid of being stranded in the middle of nowhere, and of watching the children die from thirst.

After supper eight families pulled out, heading north across the desert, along the Sublette Cutoff, maybe to reach Oregon a week earlier than the rest of us.

We no longer see buffalo or their droppings. Tall Joe says the herds have gone north and with them, the Indians.

I am somewhat pleased we may not run into them again, though it's true they haven't bothered us.

Later

Jake hit Bennie with a stick because (he says) Bennie threw sand at him. I scolded them both and made them walk the rest of the afternoon with me. Sometimes I wish they were grown-up.

Early July

After dark I walked beyond camp, around the circle to the Kenkers' wagon. A lantern lit the inside, so I stood back in the shadows to see what I could see. The mister was sound asleep, matter of fact he was snoring loud, but Mrs. Kenker was busy with something in her lap.

I stepped closer.

She had Bennie's blue sweater! She was as quick as you please unraveling the sleeve and rolling the yarn into a ball. I wanted to grab her by the throat. When did she steal Bennie's sweater and why?

I must tell Ma, even if she won't believe me. I hurried away to find her.

At the edge of the camp I saw Pepper's little

wagon. The curtains were closed and lamplight from inside made it glow like a small cozy lantern. (I feel jealous that she has a husband and I have no one yet.) How I wished she and I could watch the stars together and talk, like we did at the first of our journey. I missed her and felt more lonely than ever.

"Evening, Hattie," a voice said from the darkness.

"Who's there?" I asked.

"Come sit with us, honey." There on a blanket was Mr. and Mrs. Bigg, leaning against their wagon wheel. "We was just enjoying the sky. Why're you out here by yourself, Hattie?"

I sat with them, pulling my knees up inside my skirt for warmth as there was a cold breeze.

We were facing west. A smear of pink just above the horizon was all that was left of the sunset. Behind us, inside the circle, was campfires and singing. Folks were warming up for a dance.

After some moments I spilled out the story about Mrs. Kenker, starting with Ma's silver spoon.

They listened.

Finally Mr. Bigg said, "That poor woman." With his strong arms he pushed himself a few inches off the ground and scooted closer to his wife. She spread her shawl over their laps.

"Hattie," she said, "the Kenkers were our neighbors back in Elmcreek, Missoura. There's something you need to know about them."

Mrs. Bigg then told me that a few days before the families from Elmcreek planned to set out for Oregon, the Kenkers' house caught fire and burned to the ground. Everything was lost, all their supplies and belongings, everything. But worst of all their two grown sons died. These sons were going to drive their wagon west and help them start a new life.

"It ain't right for her to steal, Hattie, but maybe she does because she's so full of grief and empty inside."

For several minutes there was silence. The sound of crickets seemed so loud I was relieved when Mrs. Bigg spoke again. "Hattie dear, we need to think very careful how to handle this. Let's give it a few days before deciding what to do."

When I walked past the campfire back to my wagon I began to feel better for having told my story to a grown-up, so I'll not upset Ma about it. But now I feel mixed-up about the Kenkers.

July 7, Wednesday
Fort Bridger

This is as busy as Fort Laramie, but not as many Indians. Tall Joe pointed out two mountain men who were stretching beaver pelts onto circular frames.

"That one fella with the knife is Kit Carson, the scout who helped find a trail to Oregon. And that fella, that's Jim Bridger himself." Tall Joe lifted his hat in greeting when the two saw him.

"Bridger started this trading post to help emigrants, that's why it's outfitted with a blacksmith, horses, plenty of provisions, you name it. He's the first white man to see that godforsaken salt lake where Brigham Young is headed, the scoundrel."

Tall Joe blew his nose into his hand then wiped his fingers on his pants. He said, "Jim Bridger has got a map of the entire western continent stored in his brain, every river, mountain, and tree stump practically."

We camped two days here, outside the log walls. There are tears now among the women because here is where the trail splits for good. About 30 families are heading south to California, while the rest of us are going northwest for Oregon. Many friendships were made over the past three months, close friendships.

I am relieved that Pepper and I don't have to say good-bye to each other. Also, Mrs. Bigg, for I've grown very fond of her. Aside from Aunt June, she is my favorite lady friend.

Fort Bridger is also where we part ways with the Mormons. Hooray good riddance, said Tall Joe. I watched the colored fellow named Green Flake climb into his wagon and take the reins. He waved at me and smiled. Then they were gone. Pa says that next year many of the wives and children will follow.

Jim Bridger has an Indian wife. I saw her with some other squaws on the sunny side of the fort, staking down deer hides to skin. She was pretty and very young, about my age I think. I wanted to talk to her, but didn't know what to say, so instead I waved howdee. She looked down at her lap. Maybe she is shy.

Mrs. Anderson and Ma was by a creek washing our blankets. To wring them out they stood three feet apart, each holding an end and twisting until all the water dripped out. Aunt June spread them in the grass to dry. When they saw me they stopped talking, but I had already heard them.

They were saying they'd be quite content settling at Fort Bridger, never to travel again. There was water, good earth to plow, plenty of people, and all our families were safe. "Maybe Narcissa Whitman is braver than we are," Aunt June said about her friend. "I don't know how she did it."

Ma said, "And who knows what's in Oregon? Who knows what will happen between now and then? There are Indians farther north. I'm sure there's more danger that Tall Joe ain't telling us about."

Next day

Bennie's arm is healing. Pa made a new splint so it's easier for Ben to move. The other good news is that Wade is back to telling jokes. The only problems left over from the hemlock are that his tongue is numb on the right side, and his jaws ache. Tall Joe says he probably didn't eat very much of it, but Ma says it's a miracle from God, that's all there is to it, a miracle.

Mrs. Bigg called me over this morning before we pulled out from Fort Bridger. As she folded their blankets into a crate she said, "Hattie, Mr. Bigg's cart is missing. Someone took it in the night."

At noon I helped Mrs. Bigg make a search of camp. She is so large that her steps are slow. The first wagon we went to was the Kenkers'.

"I don't know what you're talking about," Mrs. Kenker said, "and how dare you accuse us, we're just poor old people, besides I'm not feeling well, neither is my husband, maybe everyone would like it if we just plumb keeled over and died before we get to Oregon, maybe y'd be happy then . . ."

Mrs. Bigg held up her hand. "That's enough,"

she said. "Go back to your nap, Mrs. Kenker, sorry to bother you."

When we were out of hearing distance I said, "If Mrs. Kenker's so innocent why did she make excuses for herself and why ain't she upset to hear someone stole Mr. Bigg's cart?"

"Hattie, if she is a thief, then soon enough she'll make a mistake and folks'll find her out. It's not like she can leave town or hide." Mrs. Bigg rested a heavy hand on my shoulder.

"Be patient, honey."

Afternoon

After a long pull up a creek called the Muddy we've come to the Bear River. There's a beautiful camp-site with a trail coming in from the right. A piece of paper was nailed to a tree. Tall Joe read it first, then passed it around.

"They made it, folks," he shouted. "The other wagons made it 'cross the desert and just a few days ahead of us seems like." Cheers went up.

Our horses, mules, oxen, and cattle are grazing

along the broad river bottom. It is the most peaceful sight. Groups of men are fishing or sitting in the sun or exploring the meadows.

There is the sound of children splashing and playing along the river. The women are spreading washed clothes on the bushes, also sitting in the sun, talking, resting. Some are busy over cooking fires.

Now it's not just Ma and Aunt June and Mrs. Anderson talking about going no farther, but several other families are discussing the very same thing: Why not settle here in the Bear River valley?

At supper five families made an announcement. This place suits them so well they've decided to homestead, said they'd not seen finer farmland ever. But Pa wants to keep going. He is so set on Oregon and living by the Pacific Ocean, he can't think of anything else.

Pa said he's had too many dreams that were lost or forgotten or that he just gave up on.

"This is our last chance, Augusta, to fulfill a dream as big as Oregon. Please stand by me. I need you."

Ma says all she dreams of is keeping her family safe. As for me, my dream is that Pepper and I will always be friends, and that I will someday be adored by a husband I love. And maybe Pepper and I can still live next door to each other!

So, we're on the trail again, ten days from Fort Hall.

Sheep Rock

One side of Sheep Rock rises up like a stone wall. Pine trees surround it on all sides and among the cliffs are mountain sheep. Tall Joe said that back in '42, John C. Frémont explored this place and named it Sheep Rock.

We're still on the Bear River. It's the same beautiful green as Pepper's eyes, and Wade's. When we saw how deep it is we were relieved to learn it makes a sharp turn south and we don't have to cross it. Tall Joe says it empties into the Great Salt Lake; he followed it once.

An amazing sight has made us all want to camp for several days. There are pools bubbling up with hot water! There's even one with a geyser called "Steamboat" because somehow it makes a high-pitched whistle that sounds just like a boat on the Missoura. Hearing it made me so happy-homesick I almost started bawling.

Folks are swimming and floating in the warm water, and drinking it. To me it smells like eggs on the rotten side, but the taste ain't bad at all.

Wade and Gideon dared each other to sit on the geyser. They took turns and, oh, what an event. While Pepper and I watched from the banks, Gideon swam out to the center and waited.

Soon enough heavy bubbles began lifting him up and up and up. His arms and legs waved like a turtle's on its back as the geyser bounced him up and down. By the time it stopped, Gideon had lost his shirt. Wade rode the geyser next and lost his pants which caused folks to erupt in hilarious laughter and so the day went.

I was so pleased to have Pepper to myself all afternoon. We lay in the grass and stared up at the clouds. I asked her what it was like to have a husband.

After a long while she turned her face toward me. How pretty she looked, her green eyes, and cheeks high with color.

"Oh, Hattie, you are such a dear. Marriage is, well, it's the most wonderful of wonderfuls. Someday you'll understand."

I wish Pepper would tell me exactly what she means, what it's really truly like to be loved by a man.

Later

At supper Ma stirred several cups of sugar and a pint of raspberries into a pail of the mineral water. Mrs. Bigg did the same with citrus syrup to make lemonade, and they was the most delicious bubbly drinks any of us had ever tasted. Pepper and I drank so much though, we were not hungry for supper, and I had a stomachache all night long. She told me the next day she did, too.

Tall Joe said one of the pools was named Beer Spring because mountain men swear they get drunk after a few sips, but Pa says that's likely just another tall tale.

Before bed

Jake and Ben complained and pushed at each other all day, then argued with me when I said it was time to unroll their blankets. I'm tired of being their sister.

Two days later

Two days north of the soda springs the sky turned black and the air cold. In an instant a wind picked up so fierce I had to hold my bonnet on with both hands even though it was tied under my chin. My skirt blew back so tight it looked like I was wearing men's trousers.

When the hail hit we stopped the wagons and ran for cover. The poor animals moaned and cried, but there was no way we could protect them. It felt like someone was pelting us with rocks. In an instant my arms and neck were bruised.

The hailstones bounced like popping corn and soon the ground was white. Many of the wagon tops, ours included, ended up with holes. The storm passed as quick as it started, and flooded the road so that mud sucked at the wheels as we pulled out.

It was our turn to be in the lead. Because of the storm we thought nothing of the abandoned wagon we came upon. Its cover also had holes.

But when Tall Joe came back from inspecting it, his face told a different story.

"Folks, those holes ain't from hailstones," Tall Joe said. He held up an arrow with feathers on its end.

Quick as you please the men began searching in case someone from the wagon was left behind. The Indians had stole the mules and whatever treasures possible, for there was a trail of scattered goods.

Wade and Gideon made a gruesome discovery. About two hundred yards away, inside a thicket of sagebrush, was a pair of feet sticking out of a grave, men's we think because they were big with hairy toes. It seems that after he was buried the Indians came back and dug deep enough to steal his boots, then left him just like we found him.

I thought it could've been Pa if *we'd* taken that shortcut. My stomach felt tight thinking Indians might be watching us and that they might not be friendly.

There was some talk about digging up the poor fellow to see who he was, but Tall Joe said it wouldn't be pretty that's for sure, and we'll likely find out when we get to Fort Hall, just a few days north.

He and Pa shoveled dirt to cover the dead man's feet and we piled rocks on top to keep animals away.

It was a solemn group that pulled out. Pepper and I and Wade walked together next to the wagon Gideon was driving. We watch the horizon more and wonder what will happen if we see Indians.

This is a land of sagebrush and rock, much of it black. Tall Joe says it is from volcanoes, and that the western part of the continent is full of them, old ones that don't erupt anymore.

Our animals pull hard and slow — they're plumb wore out. Tall Joe rides back and forth among the wagons, ordering folks to lighten their loads again. Some families pile belongings neatly to the side of the trail, others heave things out, letting them land wherever.

I keep my eye on Mrs. Kenker, but she has not thrown anything away. Two of her oxen dropped dead yesterday, one today, so now there are three pulling. Tall Joe warned her again.

"We'll leave you behind, madam, you and your junk and your husband. Better start tossing."

Every day there are at least two animals to butcher, either cows, horses, or oxen. What meat we don't eat, the women cut into strips for jerky. We hang them from the hoops inside our wagons, and the dry air toughens them pretty quick. The layers of dust seem to keep the flies and yellow jackets away.

Fort Hall

Aunt June was excited to see this trading post because Narcissa Whitman had been here and wrote to her about it. I think it looks like all the others with the usual bunch of dirty mountain men, plenty of Indians and tipis camped outside the log walls.

Pepper and I wonder if they are the same Indians that ambushed the wagons in front of us. I try not to look at them all with hatred, but it's hard not to when I think they could hurt us and women and babies, and families like ours.

We set up camp on the west side of the fort, near a creek. Tall Joe brought us news after he talked with the man in charge.

Seems the other wagons made it across the desert all right, but one of the young men stepped on a rattlesnake when he wandered into some brush. The bite is above his knee and now the poison has spread so that his entire leg is black. His fever is high.

When Tall Joe told us his name I remembered him to be one of the young men that raced us across the Platte, a loud fellow, but nice. For some reason this news made me so sick at heart I just sat on the bank staring at the water.

What next? I thought.

First it was the little twins that got lost picking berries — we still don't know if they was ever found. Then it was hemlock that killed poor Cassia, and Wade's friends . . . there was the boy who fell off his parents' wagon . . . the mother who died by Chimney Rock . . .

Suddenly my chest felt so heavy I burst out crying. Who will be next? Mama? Will Aunt June have her baby without bleeding to death? I'm tired of being brave and tired of being dirty.

I crawled in the wagon where no one could see me and took off my dress. My bare white arms are bruised from the hailstones and there are many tiny scabs from mosquito bites. My wrists and hands are dry and cracked. What boy will ever think me nice to look at?

Among the flour bags I found my satchel and the spare dress still tucked inside. I unfolded it, pulled it over my head, then tied the starched ribbon around my waist. Even though Ma said it's not to be worn until Oregon, *I do not care.* I want to feel pretty now.

Next, I undid my braid and brushed my hair one hundred strokes until at last it seemed the dust was out. For near an hour I tried to twist it on top my head like Ma does, but could not figure how, so for now will settle for a long braid.

Later

When Ma saw me wearing my clean dress she opened her mouth to say something, but instead gave me a slow smile. She opened her arms for me, then whispered, "How lovely you look, Hattie."

We stayed at Fort Hall two days. It'll be a long time before we see civilization so the men got extra parts to fix the wheels that most certainly will shrink and break in the dry air. This has been a problem since we left the Platte, many, many broken wheels. (It has been tiresome to watch so many repairs that I just have not bothered to describe them.)

The young man bitten by the rattlesnake died the evening before we pulled out. His family is devastated, but there is no time to mourn over his grave. Tall Joe says we must be going. Summer is almost over.

Next day

We are heading west along the Snake River and shall do so for about 300 miles. I have never seen such a torrent of wild water.

The river is far below us, running between black canyon walls that twist sharp here and there. Even though we're in sight of so much water, getting down to it is another matter.

Forgot to mention: Back at Fort Hall, Pa and some of the other men found enough scraps to build a cart for Mr. Bigg. The wheels are such that Mr. Bigg can roll them with his arms and get around on his own. He invited Bennie to sit on his lap for a ride and away they went, bumping through the sagebrush around the outside of the wagons, twice.

I am taking care not to scratch my arms so they won't bleed and ruin my sleeves. Aunt June gave me one of her prettiest aprons to wear over my dress. It is blue with two pockets and a ruffled hem.

Another day

Four Indians on horseback appeared out of a canyon as we were starting supper. Their dark hair was braided and their legs were bare except for moccasins. Tall Joe rode over to them with his hand raised in greeting.

The Indians, turns out, were friendly, they just wanted to warn Tall Joe about some Blackfeet who are out looking for trouble. One of the men had a bundle of fur draped over his horse's rump. He pushed it to the dirt and motioned for Tall Joe to take it. It was a buffalo skin to help our leader stay warm at night, a gift, he seemed to be saying. Tall Joe picked it up, put it around his shoulders, then walked over to his own saddlebag. He dug around in it and pulled out a small sack of tobacco which he tossed to his new friend.

I have decided Indians are like white folks in that some are honest and kind, others are liars and thieves.

After supper I almost made an awful mistake. I almost took Pa's rifle and marched over to Mrs. Kenker to give her a piece of my mind that's how mad I was.

There she was serving pie to some folks, her hair combed pretty on top her head, smiling and—of all the nerve—wearing Aunt June's other beautiful apron, the white lace one we thought we left drying on the bushes at Bear River.

The reason I did not yell at Mrs. Kenker was because Aunt June saw me thinking about it and grabbed my arm. She said, "Leave it go, Hattie."

"But it's yours . . ."

"Yes," she said, "but I think Mrs. Kenker needs it more'n I do. It's only an apron, Hattie, it ain't worth making a fuss."

But to me it ain't just an apron, it was Ma's spoon, Bennie's sweater, and all the other things.

I hate Mrs. Kenker.

She gets away with being sneaky because she's old and smiles nice and most folks is too busy to keep an eye on her, or the folks that do know her tricks keep quiet because it's easier. It's not fair. I myself am very sad that my own sisters are dead, but I don't steal from people. If I *did*, Pa would be quick to wup me and make me apologize. He don't allow dishonesty in our family.

Along the Snake River

Two days ago we passed the loudest waterfalls we've ever heard. Tall Joe says that a few years back some American trappers were in a canoe, but didn't know they was drifting toward rapids. By the time they saw how close they were it was too late to paddle backward. Over they went, drowning like bugs. That's why it's called American Falls.

Some miles later the river splits in two as it pours over a huge rock, down to a churning pool. It looks like twin waterfalls, and that's what it's called, Twin Falls.

The days are hot as ever. I must keep my sleeves down so my arms won't blister. Hour after hour the mosquitoes bite through my clothes, but I do not let myself scratch.

Another thing, the sand is too hot for us to go barefoot. My shoes split apart and the only way to keep them on is with a wet leather strip. When it dries, it shrinks tight so I can walk without them falling off.

Even so, the sand gets inside and feels lumpy. Sometimes all I can think about is how miserable I am. I wish I could be cheerful as Pepper. She never complains, and like her brother, Wade, finds a way to joke. For instance, today she looked down at her feet and laughed.

"Hattie," she said, "I bet I'm the only bride what wears her wedding shoes tied on like a bonnet."

I know this is selfish, but I'm glad Gideon is

busy all day driving their little wagon, because that means Pepper and I can talk all we want. Wouldn't Becky be surprised to learn my new best friend is a married girl!

We nooned by a creek, in a cool grove of willows. In the distance there was a rumble, like thunder, but the noise didn't stop. Tall Joe said don't be afraid, that three miles away is a waterfall so spectacular it'll take your breath away.

The families agreed to rest here an extra couple of hours and whoever wanted to see Shoshone Falls could hike in. Ma and Mrs. Anderson stayed with the littlest children and with Aunt June who's so uncomfortable she has to sleep sitting up. I think her baby will be born any day because she's big as a horse.

Jake came with us. He had trouble keeping up so Gideon and Wade took turns carrying him on their shoulders. Pepper and I had to shout because the falls were so loud we couldn't hear each other.

And, oh, what a sight. This is where the Snake River falls 200 feet over a cliff. Spray felt like rain on our faces. There were ferns and delicate flowers along the moist banks. After so many days on the desert, it was the most wonderful cool feeling, oh, how I did not want to leave. We stared for just a few minutes, then it was time to hike back to the wagons.

It seems crazy to walk six extra miles just to sightsee, but Aunt June had said, "Go, Hattie. You'll likely never have another chance."

When Pepper and I could hear ourselves again we agreed that if only we weren't in a hurry to beat winter, we'd like to stay in a place longer than a few hours.

She said, "I'm feeling tired, Hattie, like I just want to lay my head down and sleep forever."

August 1, 1847

This land is rough and dry. Prickly pear is all along the trail and beyond, much of it blooming with yellow flowers. It's pretty, but hard not to step on. We are forever picking thorns from our shoes and the hems of our skirts.

My ankles are scratched raw and have bled onto my petticoat, which can't be helped, I reckon. Like all the other women, my hem is ragged and stained with mud. There is no use trying so hard to look pretty anymore, I decided. The boys are dirty as us, worse in fact. I have not seen Pa comb his hair since Missoura, he just runs his fingers over his scalp, then puts on his hat.

Our oxen are slower each day.

After Pa talked to Ma, he took the big trunk full of my sisters' things and left it by the side of the trail. He also set out the porcelain washbowl and cabinet that had been our grandparents', Ma's wedding dress, and a box of his own tools.

I waited for Ma to break down crying, but she didn't. Ever since Pa reminded her that Oregon is our last chance to follow a dream, she has stood by him without complaint. Oh, that I could be as brave as Ma.

I opened the abandoned trunk one last time, to touch the calico my sisters had wore. How I wanted their dresses for my own, to remember them by, and also to look lovely as they had. Ma came up and gently closed the lid.

"It's time to move on, Hattie."

When the wagons pulled out it looked like we left behind a general store. There was piles of books and plates, a coffee mill, clothes, tools, and a roll-top desk. A few women wept to see their treasures thrown out. Even I had a catch in my throat. What will be left when we get to Oregon? I asked Ma. How will we make a home?

Mama said, "Don't worry, Hattie. Our home is our family, not our possessions."

When Mr. Lewis read from the Bible this morning, and after we prayed, I had a new thought about Mrs. Kenker. The farther away from Missoura we go, the more she takes. Maybe she's just scared, is all. Maybe the emptier she feels, the more she fills her wagon.

Thousand Springs

Our thermometer showed 101 degrees when we nooned. We wanted to jump in the river to cool off, but it was so far below with no way to hike down. I wish I could cut off the bottom half of my skirt for it is so hot.

On the other side of the river there was something unusual: a waterfall pouring out of a hole in the canyon wall, like a spout in a teapot. Pa said it flows from underground and is called Thousand Springs, but where it starts is a mystery.

During this stop Mr. Kenker got in another argument with Tall Joe. Soon there were fists. Uncle Tim and Pa hurried over to pull the men apart.

"Gentlemen, please, please, get a hold of yourselves," Pa said. "We have a long journey ahead of us."

But before he could say anything else, Mr. Kenker did a terrible thing. He brushed the dirt off his sleeves and said to Tall Joe, "You ain't telling me what to do anymore. It's hot and whether you like it or not I'm gonna take a swim."

Then, right before our eyes, old Mr. Kenker walked to the edge of the cliff, stepped into midair, and dropped out of sight.

For a moment there was silence, then the piercing scream of Mrs. Kenker.

Still along the Snake River

Pa says Mr. Kenker must've been going mad day by day, until finally everything got to him. After he jumped we crowded the edge on our bellies to look over. The river swept him away so fast we soon lost sight of him.

Mrs. Kenker fainted from screaming so hard and was carried to her wagon by Tall Joe himself. (I confess I am too shocked to feel sad.)

Someone spread a blanket in the shade for her. Tall Joe stood on a wheel and pulled aside the curtain to look inside. He stared for a moment, then turned toward us.

"Lordy," he said.

Two by two we peeked in and soon there was a crowd. I have never seen such junk. It was piled so high it had started to rip through the canvas.

Tall Joe said, "Go ahead, clean it out," when Pa and some others wondered what to do.

Out came Mr. Bigg's cart, the wheels gone. Mrs. Anderson claimed her quilt, Pa found his hammer, and there was the milking stool someone had given Pepper for a wedding present. I found Ma's spoon and rose plate.

I watched from a distance as folks took back their possessions. Mrs. Bigg stood next to me, also watching. Rolling her sleeves up over her big arms she said, "Hattie, as hard as it is, we need to be kind to Mrs. Kenker, whether she deserves it or not. That's what mercy is, honey."

Mrs. Kenker had recovered from her faint and was sitting up. She seemed surprised to see the contents of her wagon scattered about. Then as if she suddenly remembered what her husband had done, she covered her face with her hands and began weeping.

Tall Joe seemed beside himself. He looked at Pa, then threw his hands in the air. "Campbell, I ain't an expert in these matters. What d'you reckon we should do?"

Pa shook his head. "I dunno."

It was decided we'd spend the night where we was. Five men rode ahead to search the river for Mr. Kenker's body.

Ma and Aunt June invited Mrs. Kenker to sit with us for supper, but she stayed by her wagon instead. I'm sorry for her that she's lost her husband, even though he was a nasty fellow. How horrible that she saw him jump to his death.

Later

I think everyone's confused about how to act. For a few minutes Mrs. Kenker was treated with the tender sympathies due a widow, but moments later folks discovered she's the thief who took Mr. Bigg's cart and everything else that's been missing.

The next morning we moved out at well before sunup to beat the heat. Gideon and Wade harnessed Mrs. Kenker's two oxen and asked if she needed help loading her wagon.

"No, boys, thank you," she said quietly, not looking at them.

The last I saw of Mrs. Kenker she was sitting on a trunk surrounded by her things, looking at the river.

We must cross the Snake to get to Fort Boise. Up ahead there are three islands that Tall Joe says we'll use as stepping-stones.

His face is sunburned and looks sad. I heard him tell Pa that two years ago when he crossed here, four wagons were swept away and the families drowned.

Lord. I almost forgot how scared of rivers I am.

Before bed

After I tucked in Bennie, Jake and I sat up by the fire. He said I am his favorite sister. (He forgets I am his *only* sister.)

Fort Boise

We're almost touching the Territory of Oregon. I have not wrote for a week or so, but Aunt June says I must put it all down quick, before I forget. Good and bad.

Well, they didn't find Mr. Kenker's body. We reached Three Island Crossing mid-afternoon of the next day. Black clouds and thunder meant rain any minute. Folks discussed if we should cross now or wait for the storm to pass. While Tall Joe leaned forward in his saddle to study the river, something happened that made him decide right quick.

There came a rumbling of hooves. Indians on horseback were galloping toward us, shrieking and waving rifles. Before we could turn our wagons into a safe circle they were gone. Tall Joe shouted instructions and while word spread from wagon to wagon, the Indians made another pass. No gunfire was exchanged, but we knew they wanted us to get off their land and get off now.

(Maybe Pa would be mad, too, if strangers were tramping on our land.)

I wanted to panic, especially hearing the terrified cries of so many women and babies. I didn't know what scared me more, Indians or the thought of crossing another river.

Tall Joe led the first wagons into the water single file. The islands divide the river into four channels. Pa and Uncle Tim watched for three hours until it was our turn, the whole time nervous because the Indians had made camp a mile away and we could hear drums.

Why God sends babies into the world at times like this I'll never understand, but He does. Just as we were ready to ford this first channel Uncle Tim cried out to Ma.

"Augusta, hurry!"

Ma and I climbed into their wagon. Aunt June was lying in two inches of cold water, soaked to the skin and breathless with pain. The current was fast for I could feel us turning sideways, then pulling straight, then sideways again as the animals swam with Pa.

I was so concerned for Aunt June I quick forgot to worry about us drowning.

As we pulled up onto the first island Uncle Tim motioned to those behind us to keep going, that we'd catch up. When folks heard a baby was being born in a wet wagon, we found ourselves being given chairs, four of them, that we were able to make into a raised bed. Mrs. Lewis handed over a dry quilt, and a clean dress for Aunt June to change into.

So we crossed the second channel with water washing over our laps, but my aunt snug and dry. Her baby daughter was born just as we pulled onto the third island. Her name is River Ann Valentine.

The baby was only five minutes old when we began to ford the last channel. Screams drew Ma and me to look out the back. There was Mr. Bigg. He was tied to his seat, leaning hard to one side for his wagon was tipping over. When I saw that Mrs. Bigg had fallen in the water and was trying to grab her husband's hand, I started to leap out to help, but Ma held me back.

"Mrs. Bigg," I screamed. "Swim!"

Her arms were splashing. Each time she managed to grab a wheel or harness, the wagon tipped deeper toward her. Three men jumped in. They held on to keep it upright as another man tried to save Mrs. Bigg.

Everything happened so fast.

In an instant Mrs. Bigg and her rescuer disappeared under the tongue of the wagon. Their splashing arms were seen on the other side, moving with the river, then they were gone.

I screamed and screamed.

Mr. Bigg cried, "Sarah!" He tried to dive in after her, but couldn't get out from the rope that was holding him to the seat. His horses kept swimming and the men holding on were able to keep the wagon from sinking.

That's all I want to say for now.

Still Fort Boise

It was close to midnight by the time all the wagons made it to the other side, guided by torches we planted along shore. The reason we kept on through the darkness, made darker because clouds hid the moon and stars, was because it would have been impossible to protect ourselves the way we were spread out.

All night we could hear Indians on the south side of the river, we could see their campfires. Pa said maybe they were just trying to scare us, move us on, and wouldn't have done any harm.

Mr. Bigg invited the Anderson family to share his wagon and to help him drive. He is so heart-broken he barely speaks.

I am furious with God.

Why did someone as generous and loving and honest as Mrs. Bigg have to die while Mrs. Kenker gets to live?

The reason I know she lives is because the morning after we made the Three Island Crossing, we saw her way on the other side, trying to coax her oxen in. There were whispers about just leaving her to fend for herself.

Finally Tall Joe and Mr. Lewis swam their horses over and brought her back. She kept her eyes straight ahead and would not look at us.

I am too crushed over Mrs. Bigg to hate Mrs. Kenker anymore. I don't know why.

Afternoon

Well, to report happier news, my little cousin, River, is healthy and about the most beautiful child I've ever set eyes on. Aunt June is back to her cheerful self, walking with Ma and Mrs. Anderson. Uncle Tim made a tiny hammock to hang from inside their wagon so the baby can sleep with a cool breeze.

It bothers me that no one talks about poor Mrs. Bigg. Every time I remember her thrashing in the water my heart races with panic. If only I could have saved her . . .

I reckon the reason no one talks about her or the other terrible things that've happened is there's just not a thing in the world we can do about them.

I asked Wade his opinion on this matter, so he told me a joke. He said, "How does an ant eat a buffalo?"

"Don't know."

"One bite at a time, Hattie."

In other words, we are going to Oregon one step at a time, slowly, looking forward all the way. We must put the past behind us.

As we approached Fort Boise we found ourselves in a green valley, a welcome sight after 300 miles of black rock and desert. Woods and streams and cooler air. I tasted my first salmon, traded to us by Indians who came into camp. They were friendly and smiled easy. For once I was relaxed. It really is true, I've decided: They're as different among themselves as white folks are. I'm going to stop being afraid of them.

Just like that.

Rabbits are everywhere, so many that they're easy to hunt. We're now drying their meat like we did buffalo and ox.

Leaving Fort Boise, the Snake River turns northeast and, since we must head northwest, folks call this Farewell Bend. Tall Joe says three days from here we'll climb Flagstaff Hill. If our poor ol' wagons make it to the top we'll be able to see the Blue Mountains.

The Blue Mountains of Oregon!

Oregon.

Later

The day after Farewell Bend, Pepper's two mules died. When Gideon went looking for them in the morning, he found them lying on their sides in the grass. The sad part is there's not one spare animal left that has the strength to pull their wagon, little as it is, the rest of the way to Oregon.

Pepper and I looked inside one last time at their small collection of wedding gifts. She slipped a mirror and brush into her pocket and Gideon rolled their quilt up to carry over his shoulder.

When we reached the brow of Flagstaff Hill we were winded from the altitude and from climbing. The air was so cold my clothes felt like they wasn't on. But there in the distance, rising above a layer of clouds, were the Blue Mountains. They were covered with snow. The sight of them took my breath they were so beautiful.

I wanted to shout, "hooray," but it came out as a whisper, I was so tired.

Tall Joe slapped his hat against his leg. "We gotta move it, folks. Only 400 miles to Oregon City, but looks like winter's early. If the Blues have snow, then the Cascades surely do, too. Let's go, let's go!"

Before breakfast

My back is sore, I think from carrying Bennie yesterday. Sometimes his little legs get so tired he cries for me to pick him up.

Blue Mountains

I ain't been writing like I did when the days were hot and lazy. Guess I'm tired, guess everyone is. There've been no dances, either. We've been in the wilderness six months, but it feels like forever.

Crossing the Blues was hard on the animals. Sixteen dropped in one day, so several families were forced to abandon their wagons. Men tied ropes to the carcasses and dragged them to the side, then used planks to roll them downhill. The wagons we left as is, in case folks coming along behind us need something from them.

We butchered only five oxen as there ain't enough time to do them all. Pa hopes we'll see deer or other game.

The air has changed. It's cooler, there's moisture, I can *feel* we're in Oregon.

These mountains are thick with pine forests, with plenty of grass, water, and firewood. Pa says soil that grows trees this magnificent will grow anything. He's more and more excited, thinking about the farm we'll have. It don't bother him that we'll arrive dirty and ragged-looking.

Twins were born last night! The girl was named Sarah, after Mrs. Bigg, and the boy was named — guess! — Blue. That makes five babies on this journey, counting Eliza May.

Oh, I talked with the other bride, the one who

was instantly a mother. She is cheerful and has so much help from other women I don't think she'll figure she has four children until she wakes up in Oregon City. I asked her what it's like to have a husband. She blushed so red I thought she'd faint.

I wish for once someone would just answer my questions straight out instead of blushing!

I walk with Wade every day, but he has become more like a brother to me. My dream of falling in love seems far away now.

We are camped in a valley called Grande Ronde, surrounded by mountains. There was a loud fight after breakfast, but it was between Aunt June and Uncle Tim! Seems she had her heart set on visiting her friend Narcissa Whitman, and he says there ain't enough time.

It's here that the trail branches to the Whitman Mission at Waiilatpu, about two days north. Tall Joe said no way can we detour for a social visit.

"Winter's coming and it's coming quick," he said, agreeing with Uncle Tim.

A vote was taken. Only three families were willing to make the trip. It's too risky with snow on our heels and the Cascades to cross, plus our animals are so exhausted we may all end up walking.

Tall Joe took a stick to draw in the dirt. "Lookie here. Once you get to the Whitman Mission — I been there, I know — the only way to Oregon City is to raft down the Columbia River. The Columbia, ma'am! Do you know how many boats have sunk in them rapids? It's rough and more dangerous than the Snake, and with all these new little babies, no sir, I ain't takin' a chance."

He stood up and said to Uncle Tim, "Now, here's another idea if you don't mind spending the whole winter at Whitman's. You can come back this way next spring then follow our trail into Oregon City. That way you can avoid the Columbia, take you a month mebbe."

So we took another vote.

Funny enough, it was Aunt June who decided we should all stick together. "Narcissa will understand," she said, holding her baby against her shoulder.

Evening

This afternoon Pepper and I were tending the children and babies while their mothers washed clothes in the stream. Jake and some of his friends were sloshing along a creek that ran through our meadow. They were playing war with peashooters and whips made from plants.

For some reason I felt uneasy. I called to Jake but he ignored me, so I hurried after him. When I saw the plants the boys had pulled up I immediately grabbed Jake's toy, then did the same with the other boys'.

Their cries brought several parents running, but their angry looks vanished when I pointed to the uprooted hemlock lying in the grass.

I pulled Jake into my arms and with fear in my heart asked, "Did you eat any?"

He shook his head no. We asked the others. "No," they all said.

The hollow stems are perfect for blowing pebbles at birds, Jake explained, and also for making whistles. He pointed to three boys who'd been pretending they were smoking cigars. Their lips were numb and they felt sick to their stomachs, but they promised they hadn't eaten any.

Another search brought some girls who'd started to string necklaces with the seed pods. We threw it all into the campfire, every root, leaf, and seed. I don't know why my own brother ignored Pa's lecture from weeks ago. We showed all the kids what hemlock looks like, told them to stay away and not touch, but they didn't listen. My own brother!

Mrs. Kenker keeps to herself. One or two folks are kind, they invite her for meals, but most ignore her like she was a bug on a rock. No one has offered to drive her wagon or share a tent. It's different for Mr. Bigg. He's surrounded by people night and day, helping and comforting him. That's how much folks like him.

I miss Mrs. Bigg.

Ma says that she left behind so many kind words and memories that we'll never forget her.

"Hattie," she said when we were laying out the beds after supper, "I know two things for sure. God loves us and He has a plan for our lives. I wish

I knew why He took Mrs. Bigg and Cassia and the other children, but this I don't know."

"It ain't fair," I said, crying softly.

Ma bit her lip. She was crying, too.

Next day

Jake and Ben are sneezing and shivery. I wipe their noses with the hem of my dress and rub a little bacon grease on their chapped skin, but it's small comfort. I wish I had peppermint sticks to give them.

The Dalles

It has rained for six days. Nearly every blanket and shirt is wet. Pepper and I have undone our braids so that our hair will dry at night, but we still feel chilled and wish the sun would come out. It is miserable walking with wet clothes.

I am fed up.

Mud oozes into our poor old shoes and keeps

our feet cold. There is no way to stay warm except by rubbing our arms hard and fast. Oh, I wish I had Grandma's wool shawl to wrap around my neck and shoulders.

(While I'm feeling sorry for myself . . .) The pages of this journal are soft from the dampness which makes the pencil poke through when I try to write. It frustrates me so bad I want to throw this thing away, but Aunt June says, "Keep trying, Hattie, don't give up."

Our canvas top ripped from the wind, leaving the front hoops bare. Finally we had to throw out our other trunks and boxes, most of our cooking pots and the sacks of flour. Even the souvenir chips folks got from Chimney Rock were thrown out.

Everyone shares everything. Ma put it this way: "Why do eight women need eight dutch ovens?" She didn't blink one tear.

Such a roaring river, the Columbia. Tall Joe gave us the good news that last year a man named Samuel K. Barlow finished a road that goes around the shoulder of Mount Hood, over the Cascades, then right down into Oregon City.

"This is the first year we don't have to ride the lower end of the Columbia thank you, Jesus, amen," said Tall Joe.

It is supper. A light rain is making the fire hiss so I'll write quick, as long as my paper don't rip.

We made it up Barlow Pass, but our last two oxen that came with us all the way from Independence gave out just as we were ready to go down the western slope. The men rolled their carcasses off the trail like they did the others and we left our poor wagon under a ledge. Maybe it will be useful to next year's travelers.

Somehow now that we are on foot, I'm not so scared about things. My brothers are marching along just fine, like strong little goats. If Indians come maybe we can make friends instead of run. And with no wagon we don't have to fret about getting it across rivers. Maybe like Ma I'm becoming brave.

There was snow on the ground, but not deep.

Our footprints pressed down to mud. Wind made it unbearably cold as most of us had tossed out extra clothes like leggings and warm sweaters, and what we were wearing was damp.

I feel chilled all day and my throat is sore. My ears ache. (It is hard to write this on account of my numb fingers!)

All I can think of is how the Donner party froze and starved last winter. If we wasn't so close to our journey's end I would give up, just give up and let a bear eat me, I'm that wore out.

Two of the wagons left are driven by Mr. Bigg and Gideon, to carry the babies and littlest children and the seedlings. The rest of us walk. Pepper says she feels sick, but she keeps going anyhow, with long slow steps. When I told Ma about Pepper's illness she just smiled and told me not to worry.

Pa encourages every tired one of us. He is in such high spirits that Ma is cheerful, too. They tell my brothers and me that we are almost there.

Willamette Valley

And we are almost there! Now that we're out of the mountains we could rest a few days, but everyone's so anxious to see trail's end that we are up each dawn and moving out quicker than usual. Noon is just long enough to eat cold biscuits and drink from the stream.

It is so green everywhere, with lush pine trees. A mist makes my face feel soft again and the ends of my braids are curly. I can't see the ocean. Tall Joe said it's a few days west of Oregon City, so it's too far away to even hear the waves. He pointed north and said just across the Columbia River is Fort Vancouver, a British fur-trading post owned by Hudson's Bay Company. Soon, after we get settled, he'll take Pa there for supplies.

If only the sun would come out, even for a few minutes, we could warm up. My arms are chafed from where my wet sleeves rub, rub, rub, and there are new blisters on my feet from dampness.

Mid-October
Oregon City, here we are!

I don't know how to describe our new home. Green. Wet. Muddy.

When we finally got here it was raining. There is one broad road running through town and there are fir stumps near everywhere, enough sometimes to leap from one to another without landing in puddles.

I figured Ma and the women would fall down weeping with relief and joy that we finally really truly made it all the way to Oregon, because that's what I felt like doing.

But no. Ma looked around, asked Pa what he thought about putting our tent there. He said fine. Aunt June did the same, Mrs. Anderson, and so on. Within a few hours we had ourselves a neighborhood laid out at the edge of town.

Mr. Bigg's tent is next to the Lewis family and across the road from ours. Tall Joe is just around the bend, and the other families have spread out, too.

Tomorrow Pa will see about buying a lot. He says there must already be a few thousand folks living in Oregon City. There's two churches that we can see, four blacksmiths, a lumber mill, some saloons and stores, and many houses. There's even a school.

Pepper and Gideon are sharing our tent. Many families also are sharing until we can cut enough lumber to build homes.

I asked Ma, shouldn't we have a celebration right now, on account of finally reaching our Promised Land? But she said, no, there is too much work to be done yet. When our house is built, then we will celebrate.

October 22, 1847, Friday

I'm writing this to the sound of rain on our tent. Looks like my paper won't ever dry out so I must just get used to pressing soft with my pencil.

I still wake up in the middle of the night and wonder, Are we really here? Then I drift back to sleep, waking later to the smell of coffee and bacon frying. No bugle. No lowing cattle or creaking wagons. No dust.

No reason to hurry up and go.

Pa has already planted eight fruit trees, seedlings he bought from the Iowa brothers. He lifts his chin and closes his eyes. "Hattie," he says, breathing in deeply, "can you smell the soil, can you smell how rich it is? We'll be eating from our orchard before you know it, daughter."

October 24, 1847, Sunday

Rain crept under the tent and soaked my pillow, which is where I keep this journal. But now the back pages are so soggy they tore. I am almost at the very last page.

December 23, 1847, Thursday

It's been a long time since I wrote. We now have a cabin. There's a window that looks out to the road leading into town. I'm sitting at our new little table, on a new three-legged stool, both built by Pa. Behind me is a stone fireplace with two hens roasting and a kettle boiling for tea.

Ma and Aunt June are rolling pie dough and Pepper is by the hearth rocking River to sleep. She must practice because sometime in the spring she and Gideon will have a new baby themselves. Pa and Mr. Lewis built them a cozy room in our barn, so in a way our dream of living next door to each other has come true.

Aunt June just called over to me, her hands gooey with flour. "Remember, Hattie, tell the good and the bad."

So I will.

Last week men rode into town with news that just about broke Aunt June's heart. On November 29 her friend Narcissa Whitman was murdered, along with her husband, Marcus, and twelve others, many of them children.

We don't know the whole story, but it seems there was a measles epidemic. When some Indian children died, the Cayuse thought Dr.

Whitman was a sorcerer. So they burned down the mission.

Aunt June can't believe she'll never see her friend, the very friend who inspired her to come West in the first place. We've all talked long hours about "what if" we had gone to the mission for the winter. If we had, I wouldn't be writing this.

Ma said God's plan is bigger than us and it's impossible to guess why He lets things happen the way they do.

There's so much I don't understand.

In the two months we've been in Oregon City, the men have worked hard to put up houses. Many are still in tents, or snug under wooden lean-tos, such as Mrs. Kenker.

Somehow she managed to bring her wagon over the Blues and the Cascades. What she had in it, no one knows. Her tent is at the end of our street. Sometimes we see her walk through the mud into town, a basket on her arm. She is shunned by many of the folks from our wagon train, including me.

When Ma said she wanted to invite Mrs. Kenker to our celebration dinner I said no, absolutely no . . . not until she says she's sorry.

Ma smiled. She and Aunt June were setting the table for tea with our new cups from Fort Vancouver.

"Hattie," she said. "In order to move on we must forgive the past. Sometimes that means forgiving someone who hasn't apologized and probably never will. We don't have to forget what happened."

Ma poured boiling water into our new teapot. Squares of ginger cake sprinkled with powdered sugar were stacked on our new tin platter. Almost nothing survived our trip, just a small amount of money that Pa said is hardly worth counting, the worn-out shoes on our feet, our clothes, some blankets, my journal . . . and Ma's spoon and her little plate that I carried over the mountains in my pocket.

We've all written letters to friends in Booneville, telling them to come to Oregon. Pa rode our mail to the fort. From there the letters will go out on the next clipper ship bound for the East Coast. It'll take at least six months for them to sail south around Cape Horn, then back up to Boston, then by wagon and riverboat to Missoura.

Becky may not read my letter for another year!

Christmas, 1847

It is late and everyone's in bed. I'm writing by our new lamp — the wick is floating in whale oil that Pa got in trade from Fort Vancouver.

At noon Christmas day, our guests began arriving. Wade came with his parents, and Mr. Bigg wheeled himself over with the Andersons. He's living with them in a special room they built him. He brought a gift for each child: a small canvas sack that he cut and sewed from his old tent, each with a whistle inside that he carved from Oregon pine.

Tall Joe came with a sea captain who's staying in Portland and some neighbors who moved here a year ago. The family with the twins, Sarah and Blue, brought cranberry pies.

The last person to show up was Mrs. Kenker. She stood off by herself as if she wanted to join in, but didn't know how.

I had hoped she would arrive with gifts for all of us, by way of saying she's sorry. But she was empty-handed.

Dinner lasted four hours because we took turns with our few chairs and plates and cups — whoever wasn't eating was talking or holding a baby. During this confusion I kept my eye on Mrs. Kenker. Several times she reached down to comfort a crying child, but stopped herself, not sure if she should, I reckon. Several times she went to the kitchen to help, but seemed timid, like she didn't want to bother any of the women busy there.

She seemed so lonely, my heart began to soften. I hurried behind the curtain that hides my bed. Under my pillow is where I keep these treasures: this journal, Ma's silver spoon, and the small china plate with roses on it. I took off the sash to my apron. It is blue and about four inches wide, so I wrapped this around the spoon until it looked like a real present.

I tied it up with a piece of string and lay a fresh pine bough on top. I found Mrs. Kenker at the door just putting on her shawl. As she stepped out in the damp air I called, "Merry Christmas," then handed her my gift.

Light from the window made a patch of yellow on the ground. Gently she undid the wrapping. When she saw what it was, her eyes grew moist.

"Thank you, Hattie," she whispered. We stood there a moment in the cold. She touched my cheek, then walked to the road.

I felt good. For the first time in months I wanted to be kind to Mrs. Kenker. Maybe what Ma said yesterday is true. She said, if you "give forth" you are beginning to "for give." (But I'm not ready to part with my grandmother's plate.)

Well, I have much to think about. But before I blow out the lamp . . .

When I turned around to go back in the house, Wade was waiting for me in the doorway. He is taller than when we first met back in Missoura and tonight he wore a new cloth coat with a string tie. He was smiling when he stepped out and took my arm.

"Come on, Hattie."

We could hear music coming from the barn: There were fiddlers, and the sea captain was playing a banjo.

When I saw Mama out on the dance floor with Pa, her arm looped through his, and her head thrown back in laughter, I knew we were really truly finally in Oregon.

Just like that.

Epilogue

The families who arrived in Oregon City prospered. On May 15, 1848, Pepper and Gideon had a baby boy named Michael who was to be the oldest of seven brothers. On Christmas Eve of that year, Wade and Hattie were married. They were unable to have children of their own, but adopted the six-year-old twins, Sarah and Blue, when their parents died in a buggy crash.

For the rest of their lives Hattie and Pepper shared a fence and a vegetable garden.

The Anderson family started an inn on their fruit ranch. Mr. Bigg lived with them and became well known as a tailor and a favorite "uncle" to the many children who visited.

Mrs. Kenker lived alone in a cottage at the edge of town. One summer afternoon in 1849 Hattie went to visit, but found her dead on the kitchen floor. The constable said Mrs. Kenker had died from a heart attack at least two weeks prior.

Aunt June and Uncle Tim had three sons: Henry, Tom, and Adam who all struck out for California mining camps in search of gold. Their sister, River Ann, married Paddy O'Reilly, a famous tenor with the San Francisco Opera.

In 1906 Aunt June's granddaughter, Daisy Valentine, would be one of the survivors of San Francisco's great earthquake and fire.

Life in America
in 1847

Historical Note

Americans have always had a tradition of wanting to explore new territories and search for wide-open spaces. Today, we venture forth into the frontiers of space, and the European-American pioneers of the 1800s were no different in their spirit of adventure as they bravely set out to explore the relatively unknown parts of the North American continent.

Following a nationwide depression in 1837, there was a strong movement toward westward expansion. James Polk ran for president in 1844 as an expansionist candidate. The United States had recently gained Texas as an annexed territory (and after the Mexican War ended in 1848, California and New Mexico would become part of the country, too). The United States and Great Britain had both claimed the Oregon Territory, and Polk's campaign used the slogan, "Fifty-four-forty or fight!" This rallying cry referred to the latitude of the Oregon Territory, which America wanted to claim as its own. Ultimately, a treaty was signed with Great Britain, and the territory south of the 49th parallel — what is now Oregon and Washington — became part of America. As a result, the country nearly doubled in size during Polk's presidency.

In 1845, a newspaperman named John L. O'Sullivan used the phrase "manifest destiny" in an article he wrote about westward expansion. His theory was that since American democracy was so successful, Americans had a divine — or God-given — right to take over any land they desired, and even a duty to do so. Many citizens agreed with this philosophy, and were eager to establish homesteads on the newly acquired territories. The Indians who lived there were primarily seminomadic and believed that the land belonged to everyone. But because the pioneers had a very different cultural concept of private ownership, they claimed the land as their own, despite the fact that the Indian peoples had lived there for over ten thousand years.

The entire Oregon Trail was first used during the early part of the nineteenth century by fur trappers; missionaries; various explorers such as Jim Bridger, John C. Frémont, and Lansford W. Hastings; as well as other adventurers. The Indians had already been using parts of the trail for thousands of years. Along with the California and Sante Fe trails, the Oregon Trail served as the main route to the Pacific Ocean from the 1830s until the completion of the Transcontinental Railroad in 1869.

The two-thousand-mile-long Oregon Trail originated in Independence, Missouri, although there were several other "jumping-off points" nearby. The journey took an average of six months to complete. The first organized wagon train of fourteen wagons left from Independence in 1836. The party was led by Protestant missionaries Marcus and Narcissa Whitman and included approximately seventy men, women, and children.

Narcissa Whitman kept a detailed diary of the journey, as did many pioneer women. By 1843, the "Oregon fever" had spread, and one thousand settlers — also known as emigrants — set out on the trail. During the next few years, at least five thousand more brave pioneers followed in their tracks to settle in the rich farmland of the Oregon countryside. The Mormans, led by Brigham Young, would find their homeland around the Great Salt Lake in Utah in 1847. Countless others would head to California after gold was discovered there at Sutter's Mill in 1849.

The most famous group to travel on the Oregon Trail was the Donner Party in 1846. Eighty-nine unfortunate emigrants were stranded in the Sierra Nevada mountain range when winter arrived, preventing them from being able to complete their journey. They had left late and taken a "cutoff" — or shortcut — in order to try to save time. The decision was deadly. Many of them froze or starved to death, and the forty-seven who survived were forced to resort to cannibalism when their provisions ran out. As a result, the Donner Party became a notorious symbol of the worst that could happen during the long, dangerous journey to the Pacific Ocean. One survivor's letter to a friend back East warned, "Never take no cut ofs and hury along as fast as you can."

There were countless natural hazards to be found along the Oregon Trail. Still, more than anything else, the emigrants feared contact with Indians. But Indian attacks were actually rare. The emigrants were far more likely to die from accidents; diseases, such as cholera and typhoid; starvation; drowning while attempting a river crossing; or the perils of an unexpected blizzard. The wagon trains often encountered grass fires, hailstorms, floods, and other powerful forces of nature.

At least twenty-seven different Indian tribes lived in the areas surrounding the Oregon Trail. Some of the tribes included the Lakota Sioux, the Kiowa, the Apaches, the Pawnees, the Shoshone, the Kansa, the Arapaho, the Crow, the Cheyenne, the Bannock, and the Flatheads.

On rare occasions, Indians stole livestock or provisions from the wagon trains, but most of them were more interested in bartering with the settlers. Generally, they would provide fresh buffalo meat or salmon in exchange for cash, metal fishing hooks, calico, and other clothing items. Because the emigrants were ignorant about Indian cultures, they often behaved in an unnecessarily hostile manner toward the Indians.

Any family preparing to take the Oregon Trail needed to gather enough supplies to last for the entire journey. They would purchase or build a sturdy wagon, and buy either oxen or mules to pull it. Mules were able to travel faster, but they usually weren't strong enough to make the entire trip. Oxen could generally go only five to ten miles a day, but they were much sturdier animals. The emigrants frequently had to detour from the trail, in order to locate fresh water and plenty of grass for their animals.

Each family would stock up on lots of provisions like flour, bacon, salt pork, sugar, dried beans and fruit, saleratus (baking soda), tobacco, cornmeal, vinegar, rice, and chipped (smoked) beef. For the most part, they lived on beans and coffee, and any wild berries or root vegetables they could gather. The average breakfast consisted of bread or pancakes, fried meat, beans, and tea or coffee. There was rarely any medical care available on the trail, so they would pack primitive medicinals and remedies like laudanum (an opium medicinal) and camphor for general ailments, quinine, castor oil, and hartshorn for snakebites. The cost of the entire trip, to outfit and transport each family, was about five hundred dollars.

Most emigrants walked next to their covered wagons, rather than riding, so that the livestock would have less weight to pull, and because there was very little room to sit inside. Firewood was always scarce, and during the day, women and children collected weeds and buffalo chips (dung) to use to heat their evening meal. Though there was very little formal schooling, children learned a great deal—from how to care for animals to the names of flowers.

Women and teenage girls worked extremely

hard. In addition to cooking and caring for the younger children, they also pitched tents, built fires, drove oxen, and assumed other traditionally male duties. Some of them were pregnant during the journey, which made life even more difficult. There was never a good time to go into labor on the Oregon Trail! Women were almost always the first ones to get up in the morning to make fires and prepare breakfast, and the last people to go to sleep at night.

When the California Gold Rush hit in 1849, traffic along the first half of the Oregon Trail increased dramatically, with hundreds of thousands of people going west to seek their fortunes. By the mid-1850s, the Oregon Trail had become much safer. Ferries and bridges were common, and many trading posts were established along the way. Telegraph poles dotted the road, and some people even traveled in the relative luxury of stagecoaches and bought lodging in small inns at night. Over the years, the grueling six-month ordeal became a much safer three-month trip along smooth, well-populated roads.

Almost five hundred thousand people used the Oregon Trail between 1836 and 1870, heading to Oregon, California, and Utah. With the completion of the Transcontinental Railroad in 1869, the use of the trail was reduced to a trickle. But for many years, it was the main gateway to the West, and helped form the United States as it exists today.

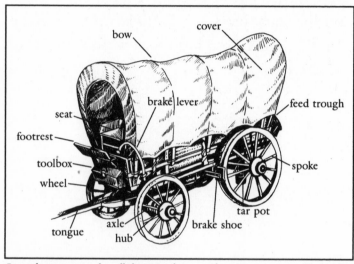

bow

cover

brake lever

feed trough

seat

footrest

toolbox

wheel

spoke

tar pot

tongue

axle

hub

brake shoe

Covered wagons were also called prairie schooners. The canvas tops were rubbed with oil to make them waterproof. Smaller front wheels helped maneuver around sharp turns, and axle grease made the wheels turn more smoothly. It took three to six yoke of oxen or four to six mules to pull each wagon.

The wagons could be as small as ten feet long and four feet wide and had to hold an entire family's food, clothing, medicines, and furniture. There were hooks inside for hanging bonnets, spoons, dolls, guns, jackets, and milk cans.

Wagons camped in circles for security, with the front of one wagon facing the back of another. Children often played inside the circle before bedtime.

185

A pioneer family after a long, exhausting day of travel. Women and girls wore skirts or dresses made from gingham and calico, sturdy shoes, and bonnets to protect them from the hot sun. Men and boys wore cotton shirts, pants made from cotton or buckskin, and wide-brimmed hats.

Women and teenage girls worked hard and became very strong physically. Here a woman gathers dried "buffalo chips," or droppings, in order to build a fire on the treeless plains. Without any of the conveniences of home, the travelers learned to be resourceful and self-sufficient.

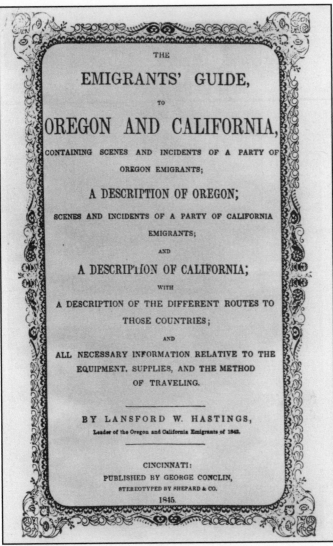

THE

EMIGRANTS' GUIDE,

TO

OREGON AND CALIFORNIA,

CONTAINING SCENES AND INCIDENTS OF A PARTY OF
OREGON EMIGRANTS;

A DESCRIPTION OF OREGON;

SCENES AND INCIDENTS OF A PARTY OF CALIFORNIA
EMIGRANTS;

AND

A DESCRIPTION OF CALIFORNIA;

WITH

A DESCRIPTION OF THE DIFFERENT ROUTES TO
THOSE COUNTRIES;

AND

ALL NECESSARY INFORMATION RELATIVE TO THE
EQUIPMENT, SUPPLIES, AND THE METHOD
OF TRAVELING.

BY LANSFORD W. HASTINGS,
Leader of the Oregon and California Emigrants of 1842.

CINCINNATI:
PUBLISHED BY GEORGE CONCLIN,
STEREOTYPED BY SHEPARD & CO.
1845.

The title page from Lansford W. Hastings's famous booklet The Emigrants' Guide, to Oregon and California. *The Donner Party followed a shortcut known as the "Hastings Cutoff," described in the book.*

The pioneers were rewarded with breathtaking scenery. But it was often so difficult to travel over the steep mountain passes that people had to discard heavier belongings, or cut their wagons down to a cart with just two wheels.

River crossings were often frightening and dangerous.

This wagon had to be abandoned when it got stuck in quicksand. Its canvas has been stripped away by strong winds.

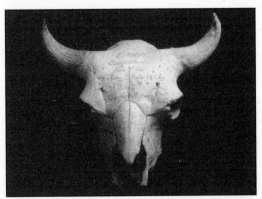

Pioneers left messages for travelers who followed behind. Sometimes they would tell them where fresh water could be found or alert them to certain dangers. This buffalo skull has a message cut into it by Brigham Young, the leader of the Mormon expedition. It says, "Pioneers camped here June 3 1847 making 15 miles today All well Brigham Young."

Water hemlock roots are so poisonous, a person could die from eating just one bite. Pioneers had to familiarize themselves with inedible plants or risk death.

Many travelers died from cholera and typhoid epidemics, as well as from accidents and natural disasters. Trailside graveyards were not uncommon sights along the way west.

A Lakota Sioux woman. Despite the emigrants' fears about Indians, the various tribes they met were mainly interested in trading. The real wars with the Indians did not begin until the 1850s and 1860s when the emigrants began to settle permanently on Indian land.

In the 1840s, thousands of buffalo roamed the plains. The pioneers relied on buffalo meat. They learned from the Indians how to jerk (dry) the meat so it would keep for long periods of time. They attached strips to their wagons and let them dry in the hot prairie sun.

JOHNY CAKE or HOE CAKE

1 pint milk
3 pints corn meal
1/2 pint flour

Scald milk and put to corn meal and flour.
Bake before the fire.

This recipe is adapted from The First American Cookbook.

SKIP TO MY LOU

With a lilt

Lost my part - ner, what - 'll I do

Lost my part - ner, what - 'll I do Lost my part - ner,

what - 'll I do Skip to my lou, my dar - ling

Flies in the buttermilk, shoo shoo shoo	I got me another one, skip, skip, skip
Flies in the buttermilk, shoo shoo shoo	I got me another one, skip, skip, skip
Flies in the buttermilk, shoo shoo shoo	I got me another one, skip, skip, skip
Skip to my lou, my darling	Skip to my lou, my darling

Words and music to "Skip to My Lou." This celebrated folk song was a favorite among pioneer teenagers. The word "lou" meant "sweetheart."

Modern map of the continental United States, showing the Oregon Trail route.

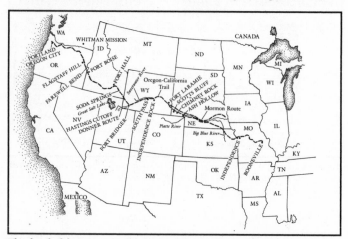

This detail of the Oregon Trail indicates important landmarks and stopping points mentioned in the diary.

About the Author

Kristiana Gregory wrote *Across the Wide and Lonesome Prairie* a few months after she and her husband and their two young sons moved from California to Colorado. "The journey itself wasn't as dangerous as Hattie Campbell's," she says. "And it took just two days instead of eight months. But like Hattie, we left behind family and lifelong friends to settle in a town we'd only seen on a map, a town where we didn't know a soul.

"I identified with the pioneers' excitement and hopes, with their dream of starting a new life in a new land. I understand the despair they must have felt to leave behind loved ones, and even though there are now telephones, fax machines, and airplanes, it is still lonely when your friends are far away. But Hattie was able to quickly begin new friendships, as we have."

Kristiana Gregory has written more than thirty

books for young readers, many in Scholastic's Dear America and Royal Diaries series, including *The Winter of Red Snow* and *Cannons at Dawn*, both Revolutionary War diaries of Abigail Jane Stewart; and *Cleopatra VII, Daughter of the Nile*; she also created the Prairie River series and Cabin Creek Mysteries series for Scholastic. Her first novel, *Jenny of the Tetons*, which was published by Harcourt, won the SCBWI Golden Kite Award for fiction. *The Winter of Red Snow* and *Cleopatra VII* were both made into movies for HBO.

In her spare time, Ms. Gregory loves to swim, read, hang out with friends, and walk her golden retrievers, Poppy and Daisy. She and her husband live in Boise, Idaho. Their two sons are all grown up.

Acknowledgments

The author would like to thank Karla J. Demby, M.D., F.A.C.P., for sharing case studies on hemlock poisoning; and Anita Tanner for historical material on Brigham Young's westward journey of 1847.

Grateful acknowledgment is made for permission to use the following:

Cover portrait by Tim O'Brien.

Cover background: A detail from William Henry Jackson's *Kanesville Crossing*, courtesy of Scotts Bluff National Monument, Nebraska.

Page 184: Wagon with parts labeled, drawing by Heather Saunders.

Page 185 (top): Interior of covered wagon, National Archives.

Page 185 (bottom): Wagons at Independence Rock,

Wyoming, Denver Public Library, Western History Collection, William Henry Jackson, WHJ-10624, Denver, Colorado.

Page 186 (top): Pioneer family, Denver Public Library, Western History Collection, artist unknown, X-11929, Denver, Colorado.

Page 186 (bottom): Frontier woman with her daughter, Bettmann/Corbis, New York, New York.

Page 187: Title page from *The Emigrants' Guide, to Oregon and California*, Library of Congress.

Page 188 (top): Wagons traveling through the Rocky Mountains, ibid.

Page 188 (bottom): Crossing the Platte River, ibid.

Page 189 (top): Abandoned wagon, National Archives.

Page 189 (bottom): Buffalo skull, The Church of Jesus Christ of Latter-Day Saints, courtesy of Museum of Church History and Art, Salt Lake City, Utah.

Page 190 (top): Hemlock, drawing by Heather Saunders.

Page 190 (bottom): Graveyard, Library of Congress.

Page 191: *She Comes Out First* by Elbridge Ayer Burbank, Collection of the Butler Institute of American Art, Youngstown, Ohio.

Page 192 (top): Buffalo, Library of Congress.

Page 192 (bottom): Recipe, adapted from *The First American Cookbook: A Facsimile of "American Cookery," 1796* by Amelia Simmons, Dover Publications, Inc., Mineola, New York.

Page 193: Words and music to "Skip to My Lou," from *The American Song Treasury* by Theodore Raph, ibid.

Page 194 (top): Map by Jim McMahon.

Page 194 (bottom): Map by Heather Saunders.

Other books in the Dear America series

DEAR AMERICA

The Diary of Emma Simpson

When Will This
Cruel War Be Over?
Gordonsville, Virginia, 1864

BARRY DENENBERG

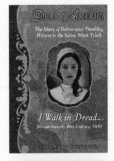

DEAR AMERICA

The Diary of Deliverance Trembley,
Witness to the Salem Witch Trials

I Walk in Dread
Massachusetts Bay Colony, 1691

LISA ROWE FRAUSTINO

DEAR AMERICA

The Diary of Abigail Jane Stewart

The Winter of
Red Snow
Valley Forge, Pennsylvania, 1777

KRISTIANA GREGORY

DEAR AMERICA

The Second Diary
of Abigail Jane Stewart

Cannons at Dawn
Valley Forge, Pennsylvania, 1779

KRISTIANA GREGORY

DEAR AMERICA

The Diary of Patsy, a Freed Girl

I Thought My Soul Would
Rise and Fly
Mars Bluff, South Carolina, 1865

JOYCE HANSEN

DEAR AMERICA

The Diary of Amelia Martin

A Light in the Storm
Fenwick Island, Delaware, 1861

KAREN HESSE

DEAR AMERICA

The Diary of Piper Davis

The Fences Between Us
Seattle, Washington, 1941

KIRBY LARSON

DEAR AMERICA

The Diary of
Remember Patience Whipple

A Journey to the
New World
Mayflower, 1620

KATHRYN LASKY

DEAR AMERICA

The Diary of Lydia Amelia Pierce

LIKE THE
WILLOW TREE
Portland, Maine, 1918

LOIS LOWRY

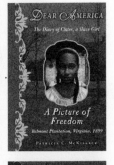

DEAR AMERICA

The Diary of Clotee, a Slave Girl

A Picture of
Freedom
Belmont Plantation, Virginia, 1859

PATRICIA C. McKISSACK

DEAR AMERICA

Diary of Catharine Carey Logan

Standing in the Light
Delaware Valley, Pennsylvania, 1763

MARY POPE OSBORNE

DEAR AMERICA

The Diary of Angeline Reddy

Behind the Masks
Bodie, California, 1880

SUSAN PATRON

DEAR AMERICA

The Diary of Dawnie Rae Johnson

With the Might
of Angels
Hadley, Virginia, 1954

ANDREA DAVIS PINKNEY

DEAR AMERICA

The Diary of Margaret Ann Brady

Voyage on
the Great Titanic
RMS Titanic, 1912

ELLEN EMERSON WHITE